The PSALMS

An inclusive language version
Translated from the Hebrew

The Grail Psalms
Available in this series

The Grail Psalms: Text only
ISBN 0 00 599682 1 (paper)

The Grail Psalms: Singing Version
ISBN 0 00 599683 X (paper)
ISBN 0 00 599665 1 (cased)

The Grail Psalms: Inclusive Language Version
ISBN 0 00 599994 4 (paper)

The Grail PSALMS

An inclusive language version
Translated from the Hebrew

COLLINS

Collins Liturgical Publications
8 Grafton St, London, W1X 3LA

Distributed in Ireland by
Educational Company of Ireland
21 Talbot St, Dublin 1

Collins Liturgical Australia
PO Box 316, Blackburn, Victoria 3130

ISBN 0 00 599994 4

First published in this edition by G.I.A. Publications
Inc, 1986
First published in this edition in the UK
by Collins Liturgical, 1986

Printed in Great Britain by Wm Collins Sons & Co,
Glasgow

INTRODUCTION

This is not a new translation of the Psalms. It is a version based on the Grail translation from the Hebrew which appeared in 1966 and is found today in liturgical books in most parts of the English-speaking world.

This version is a response by the Grail to numerous requests. It is an inclusive language version, meant for those people, certainly those women, who find the language of most of the psalms excessively masculine. For many people the constantly recurring use of words such as man, men, mankind, mortal man, brothers, sons, princes, can be a bar to the fruitful use of these ancient songs. Certainly it can make it difficult for them to see much relevance for today in these prayers.

This version has followed the same principle as the original translation, namely to pay special attention to the rhythmic structure of the poetry of the psalms. Thus this inclusive language version can also be sung, if desired, to the melodies of Joseph Gelineau, SJ, for which full music editions are available.

In the original translation the numbering of the psalms was taken from the Greek Septuagint. In this edition, those numbers appear in parentheses followed by the Hebrew number.

1. The two ways

1 Happy indeed are those
who follow not the counsel of the wicked,
nor linger in the way of sinners
nor sit in the company of scorners,
2 but whose delight is the law of the Lord
and who ponder his law day and night.

3 They are like a tree that is planted
beside the flowing waters,
that yields its fruit in due season
and whose leaves shall never fade;
and all that they do shall prosper.
4 Not so are the wicked, not so!

For they like winnowed chaff
shall be driven away by the wind.
5 When the wicked are judged they shall not stand,
nor find room among those who are just;
6 for the Lord guards the way of the just
but the way of the wicked leads to doom.

2. God's chosen king

1 Why this tumult among nations,
among peoples this useless murmuring?
2 They arise, the kings of the earth,
princes plot against the Lord and his Anointed.
3 "Come, let us break their fetters,
come, let us cast off their yoke."

4 He who sits in the heavens laughs,
the Lord is laughing them to scorn.
5 Then he will speak in his anger,
his rage will strike them with terror.
6 "It is I who have set up my king
on Zion, my holy mountain."

7 (I will announce the decree of the Lord.)

The Lord said to me: "You are my Son.
It is I who have begotten you this day.
8 Ask and I shall bequeath you the nations,
put the ends of the earth in your possession.
9 With a rod of iron you will break them,
shatter them like a potter's jar."

10 Now, O kings, understand,
take warning, rulers of the earth;
11 serve the Lord with awe
and trembling, pay him your homage
12 lest he be angry and you perish;
for suddenly his anger will blaze.

Blessed are they who put their trust in God.

3. A morning prayer for help

2 How many are my foes, O Lord!
How many are rising up against me!
3 How many are saying about me:
"No help will come from God."

4 But you, Lord, are a shield about me,
my glory, who lift up my head.
5 I cry aloud to you, Lord.
You answer from your holy mountain.

6 I lie down to rest and I sleep.
I wake, for you uphold me.
7 I will not fear even thousands of people
who are ranged on every side against me.

8 Arise, Lord; save me, my God,
you who strike all my foes on the mouth,
you who break the teeth of the wicked!
9 O Lord of salvation, bless your people!

4. Night prayer

2 When I call, answer me, O God of justice;
from anguish you released me, have mercy
and hear me!

3 You rebels, how long will your hearts be closed,
will you love what is futile and seek what is false?

4 It is the Lord who grants favors to those whom
he loves;
the Lord hears me whenever I call him.

5 Fear him; do not sin: ponder on your bed
and be still.
6 Make justice your sacrifice and trust in the Lord.

7 "What can bring us happiness?" many say.
Lift up the light of your face on us, O Lord.

8 You have put into my heart a greater joy
than they have from abundance of corn
and new wine.

9 I will lie down in peace and sleep comes at once
for you alone, Lord, make me dwell in safety.

5. Morning prayer

2 To my words give ear, O Lord,
give heed to my groaning.
3 Attend to the sound of my cries,
4 my King and my God.

It is you whom I invoke, 4 O Lord.
In the morning you hear me;
in the morning I offer you my prayer,
watching and waiting.

5 You are no God who loves evil;
no sinner is your guest.
6 The boastful shall not stand their ground
before your face.

7 You hate all who do evil;
you destroy all who lie.
Deceitful and bloodthirsty people
are hateful to you, Lord.

8 But I through the greatness of your love
have access to your house.
I bow down before your holy temple,
filled with awe.

9 Lead me, Lord, in your justice,
because of those who lie in wait;
make clear your way before me.

10 No truth can be found in their mouths,
their heart is all mischief,
their throat a wide-open grave,
all honey their speech.

11 Declare them guilty, O God.
Let them fail in their designs.
Drive them out for their many offenses,
for they have defied you.

12 All those you protect shall be glad
and ring out their joy.
You shelter them; in you they rejoice,
those who love your name.

13 Lord, it is you who bless the upright:
you surround them with favor as with a shield.

6. A prayer in time of need

2 Lord, do not reprove me in your anger;
punish me not, in your rage.
3 Have mercy on me, Lord, I have no strength;
Lord, heal me, my body is racked,
4 my soul is racked with pain.

But you, O Lord . . . how long?
5 Return, Lord, rescue my soul.
Save me in your merciful love;
6 for in death no one remembers you;
from the grave, who can give you praise?

7 I am exhausted with my groaning;
every night I drench my pillow with tears;
I bedew my bed with weeping.
8 My eye wastes away with grief;
I have grown old surrounded by my foes.

9 Leave me, all you who do evil,
for the Lord has heard my weeping.
10 The Lord has heard my plea,
the Lord will accept my prayer.
11 All my foes will retire in confusion,
foiled and suddenly confounded.

7. A prayer for justice

2 Lord God, I take refuge in you.
From my pursuers save me and rescue me,
3 lest they tear me to pieces like a lion
and drag me off with no one to rescue me.

4 Lord God, if my hands have done wrong,
5 if I have paid back evil for good,
I who saved my unjust oppressor:
6 then let my foes pursue me and seize me,
let them trample my life to the ground
and lay my soul in the dust.

* * * * *

7 Lord, rise up in your anger,
rise against the fury of my foes;
my God, awake! You will give judgement.
8 Let the company of nations gather round you,
taking your seat above them on high.
9 (The Lord is judge of the peoples.)

Give judgment for me, Lord; I am just
and innocent of heart.

10 Put an end to the evil of the wicked!
Make the just stand firm,
you who test mind and heart,
O just God!

11 God is the shield that protects me,
who saves the upright of heart.
12 God is a just judge
slow to anger;
but he threatens the wicked every day,
13 all those who will not repent.

* * * * *

God will sharpen his sword;
he has braced his bow and taken aim.
14 For them he has prepared deadly weapons;
he barbs his arrows with fire.
15 Here are enemies pregnant with malice,
who conceive evil and bring forth lies.

16 They dig a pitfall, dig it deep;
and in the trap they have made they will fall.
17 Their malice will recoil on themselves;
on their own heads their violence will fall.

* * * * *

18 I will thank the Lord for his justice:
I will sing to the Lord, the Most High.

8. Divine glory and human dignity

2 How great is your name, O Lord our God,
through all the earth!

Your majesty is praised above the heavens;
3 on the lips of children and of babes
you have found praise to foil your enemy,
to silence the foe and the rebel.

4 When I see the heavens, the work of your hands,
the moon and the stars which you arranged,
5 what are we that you should keep us in mind,
men and women that you care for us?

6 Yet you have made us little less than gods;
and crowned us with glory and honor,
7 gave us power over the works of your hands,
put all things under our feet.

8 All of them, sheep and cattle,
yes, even the savage beasts,
9 birds of the air, and fish
that make their way through the waters.

10 How great is your name, O Lord our God
through all the earth!

9. Gratitude and appeal

2 I will praise you, Lord, with all my heart;
I will recount all your wonders.
3 I will rejoice in you and be glad,
and sing psalms to your name, O Most High.

4 See how my enemies turn back,
how they stumble and perish before you.
5 You upheld the justice of my cause;
you sat enthroned, judging with justice.

6 You have checked the nations, destroyed
the wicked;
you have wiped out their name for ever and ever.
7 The foe is destroyed, eternally ruined.
You uprooted their cities; their memory has
perished.

8 But the Lord sits enthroned for ever.
He has set up his throne for judgment;
9 he will judge the world with justice,
he will judge the peoples with his truth.

10 For the oppressed let the Lord be a stronghold,
a stronghold in times of distress.
11 Those who know your name will trust you;
you will never forsake those who seek you.

12 Sing psalms to the Lord who dwells in Zion.
Proclaim his mighty works among the peoples,
13 for the Avenger of blood has remembered them,
has not forgotten the cry of the poor.

14 Have pity on me, Lord, see my sufferings,
you who save me from the gates of death;
15 that I may recount all your praise
at the gates of the city of Zion
and rejoice in your saving help.

16 The nations have fallen in the pit which they made,
their feet caught in the snare they laid.
17 The Lord has revealed himself, and given
judgment.
The wicked are snared in the work of their
own hands.

18 Let the wicked go down among the dead,
all the nations forgetful of God;
19 for the needy shall not always be forgotten
nor the hopes of the poor be in vain.

20 Arise, Lord, let mortals not prevail!
Let the nations be judged before you.
21 Lord, strike them with terror,
let the nations know they are but mortals.

(9b) 10. A prayer for justice

1 Lord, why do you stand afar off
and hide yourself in times of distress?
2 The poor are devoured by the pride of the wicked;
they are caught in the schemes that others
have made.

3 For the wicked boast of their heart's desires;
the covetous blaspheme and spurn the Lord.
4 In their pride the wicked say: "God will not
punish.
There is no God." Such are their thoughts.

5 Their path is ever untroubled;
your judgment is far from their minds.
Their enemies they regard with contempt.
6 They think: "Never shall we falter:
misfortune shall never be our lot."

7 Their mouths are full of cursing, guile, oppression;
mischief and deceit are their food.
8 They lie in wait among the reeds;
they murder the innocent in secret.

Their eyes are on the watch for the helpless.
9 They lurk in hiding like lions in their den;
they lurk in hiding to seize the poor;
they seize the poor and drag them away.

10 They crouch, preparing to spring,
and the helpless fall beneath such strength.
11 They think in their hearts: "God forgets,
he hides his face, he does not see."

12 Arise then, Lord, lift up your hand!
O God, do not forget the poor!
13 Why should the wicked spurn the Lord
and think in their hearts: "God will not punish?"

14 But you have seen the trouble and sorrow,
you note it, you take it in hand.
The helpless entrust themselves to you,
for you are the helper of the orphan.

15 Break the power of the wicked and the sinner!
Punish their wickedness till nothing remains!
16 The Lord is king for ever and ever.
The heathen shall perish from the land he rules.

17 Lord, you hear the prayer of the poor;
you strengthen their hearts; you turn your ear
18 to protect the rights of the orphan and oppressed
so that earthly tyrants may strike terror no more.

(10) 11. Tne security of God's friends

1 In the Lord I have taken my refuge.
How can you say to my soul:
"Fly like a bird to its mountain.

2 See the wicked bracing their bow;
they are fixing their arrows on the string
to ambush the upright by stealth.
3 Foundations once destroyed, what can
the just do?"

4 The Lord is in his holy temple,
the Lord, whose throne is in heaven.
His eyes look down on the world;
his gaze tests the people of the earth.

5 The Lord tests the just and the wicked;
the lover of violence he hates.
6 He sends fire and brimstone on the wicked;
he sends a scorching wind as their lot.

7 The Lord is just and loves justice;
the upright shall see his face.

(11) 12. A prayer for help

2 Help, O Lord, for the faithful have vanished;
truth has gone from the people of the earth.
3 Falsehood they speak one to another,
with lying lips, with a false heart.

4 May the Lord destroy all lying lips,
the tongue that speaks high-sounding words,
5 those who say: "Our tongue is our strength;
our lips are our own, who is our ruler?"

"For the poor who are oppressed and the
needy who groan
I myself will arise," says the Lord,
"I will grant them the salvation for which
they thirst."

7 The words of the Lord are words without alloy,
silver from the furnace, seven times refined.

8 It is you, O Lord, who will take us in your care
and protect us for ever from this generation.
9 See how the wicked prowl on every side,
and worthless men and women are praised
to the skies.

(12) 13. A prayer of one in anxiety

2 How long, O Lord, will you forget me?
How long will you hide your face?
3 How long must I bear grief in my soul,
this sorrow in my heart day and night?
How long shall my enemy prevail?

4 Look at me, answer me, Lord my God!
Give light to my eyes lest I fall asleep in death,
5 lest my enemy say: "I have prevailed";
lest my foes rejoice to see my fall.

6 As for me, I trust in your merciful love.
Let my heart rejoice in your saving help.
7 Let me sing to the Lord for his goodness to me,
singing psalms to the name of the Lord, the
Most High.

(13) 14. Fools

1 Fools have said in their hearts:
"There is no God above."
Their deeds are corrupt, depraved;
there is no good person left.

2 From heaven the Lord looks down
on the people of the earth
to see if any are wise,
if any seek God.

3 All have left the right path,
depraved, every one;
there is no good person left,
no, not even one.

4 Will the evil-doers not understand?
They eat up my people
as though they were eating bread;
they never pray to the Lord.

5 See how they tremble with fear
without cause for fear,
for God is with the just.
6 You may mock the hope of the poor
but their refuge is the Lord.

7 O that Israel's salvation might come from Zion!
When the Lord delivers his people from bondage,
then Jacob will be glad and Israel rejoice.

See psalm (52) 53

(14) 15. Who can stand before the Lord?

1 Lord, who shall be admitted to your tent
and dwell on your holy mountain?

2 Those who walk without fault,
those who act with justice
and speak the truth from their hearts,
3 those who do not slander with their tongue,

those who do no wrong to their kindred,
who cast no slur on their neighbors,
4 who hold the godless in disdain,
but honor those who fear the Lord;

those who keep their word, come what may,
5 who take no interest on a loan
and accept no bribes against the innocent.
Such people will stand firm for ever.

(15) 16. True happiness

1 Preserve me, God, I take refuge in you.
2 I say to you Lord: "You are my God.
My happiness lies in you alone."

3 You have put into my heart a marvelous love
for the faithful ones who dwell in your land.
4 Those who choose other gods increase
their sorrows.
Never will I offer their offerings of blood.
Never will I take their name upon my lips.

5 O Lord, it is you who are my portion and cup,
it is you yourself who are my prize.
6 The lot marked out for me is my delight,
welcome indeed the heritage that falls to me!

7 I will bless you, Lord, you give me counsel,
and even at night direct my heart.
8 I keep you, Lord, ever in my sight;
since you are at my right hand, I shall stand firm.

9 And so my heart rejoices, my soul is glad;
even my body shall rest in safety.
10 For you will not leave my soul among the dead,
nor let your beloved know decay.

11 You will show me the path of life,
the fullness of joy in your presence,
at your right hand happiness for ever.

(16) 17. A prayer of an innocent person

1 Lord, hear a cause that is just,
pay heed to my cry.
Turn your ear to my prayer,
no deceit is on my lips.

2 From you may my judgment come forth.
Your eyes discern the truth.

3 You search my heart, you visit me by night.
You test me and you find in me no wrong.
My words are not sinful 4 like human words.

I kept from violence because of your word,
5 I kept my feet firmly in your paths;
there was no faltering in my steps.

6 I am here and I call, you will hear me, O God.
Turn your ear to me; hear my words.
7 Display your great love, you whose right hand saves
your friends from those who rebel against them.

8 Guard me as the apple of your eye.
Hide me in the shadow of your wings
9 from the violent attack of the wicked.

My foes encircle me with deadly intent.
10 Their hearts tight shut, their mouths speak proudly.
11 They advance against me, and now they surround me.

Their eyes are watching to strike me to the ground,
12 as though they were lions ready to claw
or like some young lion crouched in hiding.

13 Lord, arise, confront them, strike them down!
Let your sword rescue my soul from the wicked;
14 let your hand, O Lord, rescue me from the enemy,
from those whose reward is in this present life.

You give them their fill of your treasures;
they rejoice in abundance of offspring
and leave their wealth to their children.

15 As for me, in my justice I shall see your face
and be filled, when I awake, with the sight of your glory.

(17) 18. David's song of victory

2 I love you, Lord, my strength,
3 my rock, my fortress, my savior.
God, you are the rock where I take refuge;
my shield, my mighty help, my stronghold.
4 Lord, you are worthy of all praise,
when I call I am saved from my foes.

5 The waves of death rose about me;
the torrents of destruction assailed me;
6 the snares of the grave entangled me;
the traps of death confronted me.

7 In my anguish I called to you, Lord;
I cried to you, God, for help.
From your temple you heard my voice;
my cry came to your ears.

8 Then the earth reeled and rocked;
the mountains were shaken to their base,
they reeled at your terrible anger.
9 Smoke came forth from your nostrils
and scorching fire from your mouth,
coals were set ablaze by its heat.

10 You lowered the heavens and came down,
a black cloud under your feet.
11 You came enthroned on the cherubim,
you flew on the wings of the wind.

12 You made the darkness your covering,
the dark waters of the clouds, your tent.
13 A brightness shone out before you
with hailstones and flashes of fire.

14 Lord, you thundered in the heavens,
Most High, you let your voice be heard.
15 You shot your arrows, scattered the foe,
flashed your lightnings and put them to flight.

16 The bed of the ocean was revealed;
the foundations of the world were laid bare
at the thunder of your threat, O Lord,
at the blast of the breath of your anger.

17 From on high you reached down and seized me;
you drew me forth from the mighty waters.
18 You snatched me from my powerful foe,
from my enemies whose strength I could
not match.

19 They assailed me in the day of my misfortune,
but you, Lord, were my support.
20 You brought me forth into freedom,
you saved me because you loved me.

21 You rewarded me because I was just,
repaid me, for my hands were clean,
22 for I have kept your way, O Lord,
and have not fallen away from you.

23 For your judgments are all before me;
I have never neglected your commands.
24 I have always been upright before you;
I have kept myself from guilt.

25 You repaid me because I was just
and my hands were clean in your eyes.
26 You are loving with those who love you,
you show yourself perfect with the perfect.

27 With the sincere you show yourself sincere,
but the cunning you outdo in cunning.
28 For you save a humble people
but humble the eyes that are proud.

29 You, O Lord, are my lamp,
my God who lightens my darkness.
30 With you I can break through any barrier,
with my God I can scale any wall.

31 Your ways, O God, are perfect;
your word, O Lord, is purest gold.
You indeed are the shield
of all who make you their refuge.

32 For who is God but you, Lord?
Who is a rock but you, my God?
33 You who gird me with strength
and make the path safe before me.

34 My feet you made swift as the deer's,
you have made me stand firm on the heights.
35 You have trained my hands for battle
and my arms to bend the heavy bow.

36 You gave me your saving shield;
you upheld me, trained me with care.
37 You gave me freedom for my steps;
my feet have never slipped.

38 I pursued and overtook my foes,
never turning back till they were slain.
39 I smote them so they could not rise;
they fell beneath my feet.

40 You girded me with strength for battle,
you made my enemies fall beneath me,
41 you made my foes take flight;
those who hated me I destroyed.

42 They cried, but there was no one to save them;
they cried to you, Lord, but in vain.
43 I crushed them fine as dust before the wind;
trod them down like dirt in the streets.

44 You saved me from the feuds of the people
and put me at the head of the nations.
45 People unknown to me served me;
when they heard of me they obeyed me.

Foreign nations came to me cringing,
46 foreign nations faded away.
They came trembling out of their strongholds.

47 Long life to you, Lord, my rock!
Praise to you, God, who saves me,
48 the God who gives me redress
and subdues people under me.

49 You saved me from my furious foes.
You set me above my assailants.
You saved me from violent hands,
50 so I will praise you, Lord, among the nations;
I will sing a psalm to your name.

51 You have given great victories to your king
and shown your love for your anointed,
for David and his line for ever.

(18) 19. Praise for the Lord, creator of all

2 The heavens proclaim your glory, O God,
and the firmament shows forth the work
of your hands.
3 Day unto day takes up the story
and night unto night makes known the message.

4 No speech, no word, no voice is heard
5 yet their span extends through all the earth,
their words to the utmost bounds of the world.

There you have placed a tent for the sun;
6 it comes forth like a bridegroom coming from
his tent,
rejoices like a champion to run its course.

7 At the end of the sky is the rising of the sun;
to the furthest end of the sky is its course.
There is nothing concealed from its burning heat.

* * * * *

8 The law of the Lord is perfect,
it revives the soul.
The rule of the Lord is to be trusted,
it gives wisdom to the simple.

9 The precepts of the Lord are right,
they gladden the heart.
The command of the Lord is clear,
it gives light to the eyes.

10 The fear of the Lord is holy,
abiding for ever.
The decrees of the Lord are truth
and all of them just.

11 They are more to be desired than gold,
than the purest of gold
and sweeter are they than honey,
than honey from the comb.

12 So in them your servant finds instruction;
great reward is in their keeping.
13 But can we discern all our errors?
From hidden faults acquit us.

14 From presumption restrain your servant
and let it not rule me.
Then shall I be blameless,
clean from grave sin.

15 May the spoken words of my mouth,
the thoughts of my heart,
win favor in your sight, O Lord,
my rescuer, my rock!

(19) 20. A prayer before battle

2 May the Lord answer in time of trial;
may the name of Jacob's God protect you.

3 May he send you help from his shrine
and give you support from Zion.
4 May he remember all your offerings
and receive your sacrifice with favor.

5 May he give you your heart's desire
and fulfill every one of your plans.
6 May we ring out our joy at your victory
and rejoice in the name of our God.
May the Lord grant all your prayers.

7 I am sure now that the Lord
will give victory to his anointed,
will reply from his holy heaven
with the mighty victory of his hand.

8 Some trust in chariots or horses,
but we in the name of the Lord.
9 They will collapse and fall,
but we shall hold and stand firm.

10 Give victory to the king, O Lord,
give answer on the day we call.

(20) 21. Thanksgiving for victory

2 O Lord, your strength gives joy to the king;
how your saving help makes him glad!
3 You have granted him his heart's desire;
you have not refused the prayer of his lips.

4 You came to meet him with the blessings of
success;
you have set on his head a crown of pure gold.
5 He asked you for life and this you have given,
days that will last from age to age.

6 Your saving help has given him glory.
You have laid upon him majesty and splendor,
7 you have granted your blessings to him for ever.
You have made him rejoice with the joy of your
presence.

8 The king has put his trust in the Lord;
through the mercy of the Most High he shall
stand firm.
9 His hand will seek and find all his foes,
his right hand find out those that hate him.

10 You will burn them like a blazing furnace
on the day when you appear.
And the Lord shall destroy them in his anger;
fire will swallow them up.

11 You will wipe out their offspring from the earth
and their children from among its peoples.
12 Though they plan evil against you,
though they plot, they shall not prevail.

13 For you will force them to retreat;
at them you will aim with your bow.
14 O Lord, arise in your strength;
we shall sing and praise your power.

(21) 22. The just one in distress

2 My God, my God, why have you forsaken me?
You are far from my plea and the cry of my
distress.
3 O my God, I call by day and you give no reply;
I call by night and I find no peace.

4 Yet you, O God, are holy,
enthroned on the praises of Israel.
5 In you our forebears put their trust;
they trusted and you set them free.
6 When they cried to you, they escaped.
In you they trusted and never in vain.

7 But I am a worm and no man,
the butt of all, laughing-stock of the people.
8 All who see me deride me.
They curl their lips, they toss their heads.
9 "He trusted in the Lord, let him save him;
let him release him if this is his friend."

10 Yes, it was you who took me from the womb,
entrusted me to my mother's breast.
11 To you I was committed from my birth,
from my mother's womb you have been my God.

12 Do not leave me alone in my distress;
Come close, there is none else to help.

13 Many bulls have surrounded me,
fierce bulls of Bashan close me in.
14 Against me they open wide their jaws,
like lions, rending and roaring.

15 Like water I am poured out,
disjointed are all my bones.
My heart has become like wax,
it is melted within my breast.

16 Parched as burnt clay is my throat,
my tongue cleaves to my jaws.

17 Many dogs have surrounded me,
a band of the wicked beset me.
They tear holes in my hands and my feet
16c and lay me in the dust of death.

18 I can count every one of my bones.
These people stare at me and gloat;
19 they divide my clothing among them.
They cast lots for my robe.

20 O Lord, do not leave me alone,
my strength, make haste to help me!
21 Rescue my soul from the sword,
my life from the grip of these dogs.
22 Save my life from the jaws of these lions,
my poor soul from the horns of these oxen.

23 I will tell of your name to my people
and praise you where they are assembled.
24 "You who fear the Lord give him praise;
all children of Jacob, give him glory.
Revere him, children of Israel.

25 For he has never despised
nor scorned the poverty of the poor.
From them he has not hidden his face,
but he heard the poor when they cried."

26 You are my praise in the great assembly.
My vows I will pay before those who fear him.
27 The poor shall eat and shall have their fill.
They shall praise the Lord, those who seek him.
May their hearts live for ever and ever!

28 All the earth shall remember and return to
the Lord,
all families of the nations worship before him;
29 for the kingdom is the Lord's, he is ruler of
the nations.
30 They shall worship him, all the mighty of
the earth;
before him shall bow all who go down to
the dust.

And my soul shall live for him, 31 my children serve him.
They shall tell of the Lord to generations yet to come,
32 declare his faithfulness to peoples yet unborn:
"These things the Lord has done."

(22) 23. God, shepherd and host

1 The Lord is my shepherd;
there is nothing I shall want.
2 Fresh and green are the pastures
where he gives me repose.
Near restful waters he leads me,
3 to revive my drooping spirit.

He guides me along the right path;
he is true to his name.
4 If I should walk in the valley of darkness
no evil would I fear.
You are there with your crook and your staff;
with these you give me comfort.

5 You have prepared a banquet for me
in the sight of my foes.
My head you have anointed with oil;
my cup is overflowing.

6 Surely goodness and kindness shall follow me
all the days of my life.
In the Lord's own house shall I dwell
for ever and ever.

(23) 24. The Lord of glory

1 The Lord's is the earth and its fullness,
the world and all its peoples.
2 It is he who set it on the seas;
on the waters he made it firm.

3 Who shall climb the mountain of the Lord?
Who shall stand in his holy place?
4 Those with clean hands and pure heart,
who desire not worthless things,
(who have not sworn so as to deceive their
neighbor.)

5 They shall receive blessings from the Lord
and reward from the God who saves them.
6 These are the ones who seek him,
seek the face of the God of Jacob.

* * * * *

7 O gates, lift high your heads;
grow higher, ancient doors.
Let him enter, the king of glory!

8 Who is the king of glory?
The Lord, the mighty, the valiant,
the Lord, the valiant in war.

9 O gates, lift high your heads;
grow higher, ancient doors.
Let him enter, the king of glory!

10 Who is he, the king of glory?
He, the Lord of armies,
he is the king of glory.

(24) 25. A prayer for guidance and protection

1 To you, O Lord, I lift up my soul.
2 I trust you, let me not be disappointed;
do not let my enemies triumph.
3 Those who hope in you shall not be disappointed,
but only those who wantonly break faith.

4 Lord, make me know your ways.
Lord, teach me your paths.
5 Make me walk in your truth, and teach me,
for you are God my savior.

In you I hope all day long
7c because of your goodness, O Lord.
6 Remember your mercy, Lord,
and the love you have shown from of old.
7 Do not remember the sins of my youth.
In your love remember me.

8 The Lord is good and upright.
He shows the path to those who stray,
9 He guides the humble in the right path,
He teaches his way to the poor.

10 His ways are faithfulness and love
for those who keep his covenant and will.
11 Lord, for the sake of your name
forgive my guilt, for it is great.

12 To those who revere the Lord
he will show the path they should choose.
13 Their souls will live in happiness
and their children shall possess the land.
14 The Lord's friendship is for those who revere him;
to them he reveals his covenant.

15 My eyes are always on the Lord,
for he rescues my feet from the snare.
16 Turn to me and have mercy
for I am lonely and poor.

17 Relieve the anguish of my heart
and set me free from my distress.
18 See my affliction and my toil
and take all my sins away.

19 See how many are my foes,
how violent their hatred for me.
20 Preserve my life and rescue me.
Do not disappoint me, you are my refuge.
21 May innocence and uprightness protect me,
for my hope is in you, O Lord.

22 Redeem Israel, O God, from all its distress.

(25) 26. Confidence in God

1 Give judgment for me, O Lord,
for I walk the path of perfection.
I trust in the Lord; I have not wavered.

2 Examine me, Lord, and try me;
O test my heart and my mind,
3 for your love is before my eyes
and I walk according to your truth.

4 I never take my place with liars
and with hypocrites I shall not go.
5 I hate the evildoer's company;
I will not take my place with the wicked.

6 To prove my innocence I wash my hands
and take my place around your altar,
7 singing a song of thanksgiving,
proclaiming all your wonders.

8 O Lord, I love the house where you dwell,
the place where your glory abides.

9 Do not sweep me away with sinners,
nor my life with bloodthirsty people
10 in whose hands are evil plots,
whose right hands are filled with gold.

11 As for me, I walk the path of perfection.
Redeem me and show me your mercy.
12 My foot stands on level ground;
I will bless the Lord in the assembly.

(26) 27. Trust in time of affliction

1 The Lord is my light and my help;
who shall I fear?
The Lord is the stronghold of my life;
before whom shall I shrink?

2 When evildoers draw near
to devour my flesh,
it is they, my enemies and foes,
who stumble and fall.

3 Though an army encamp against me
my heart would not fear.
Though war break out against me
even then would I trust.

4 There is one thing I ask of the Lord,
for this I long,
to live in the house of the Lord,
all the days of my life,
to savor the sweetness of the Lord,
to behold his temple.

5 For there he keeps me safe in his tent
in the day of evil.
He hides me in the shelter of his tent,
on a rock he sets me safe.

6 And now my head shall be raised
above my foes who surround me
and I shall offer within his tent
a sacrifice of joy.

I will sing and make music for the Lord.

7 O Lord, hear my voice when I call;
have mercy and answer.
8 Of you my heart has spoken:
"Seek his face."

It is your face, O Lord, that I seek;
9 hide not your face.
Dismiss not your servant in anger;
you have been my help.

Do not abandon or forsake me,
O God my help!
10 Though father and mother forsake me,
the Lord will receive me.

11 Instruct me, Lord, in your way;
on an even path lead me.
When they lie in ambush 12 protect me
from my enemy's greed.
False witnesses rise against me,
breathing out fury.

13 I am sure I shall see the Lord's goodness
in the land of the living.
14 Hope in him, hold firm and take heart.
Hope in the Lord!

(27) 28. A prayer in time of danger

1 To you, O Lord, I call,
my rock, hear me.
If you do not heed I shall become
like those in the grave.

2 Hear the voice of my pleading
as I call for help,
as I lift up my hands in prayer
to your holy place.

3 Do not drag me away with the wicked,
with the evildoers,
who speak words of peace to their neighbors
but with evil in their hearts.

4 Repay them as their actions deserve
and the malice of their deeds.
Repay them for the work of their hands;
give them their deserts.
5 For they ignore your deeds, O Lord,
and the work of your hands.
(May you ruin them and never rebuild them.)

6 Praise to you, Lord, you have heard
my cry, my appeal.
7 You, Lord, are my strength and my shield;
in you my heart trusts.
I was helped, my heart rejoices
and I praise you with my song.

8 Lord, you are the strength of your people,
a fortress where your anointed find help.
9 Save your people; bless Israel your heritage.
Be their shepherd and carry them for ever.

(28) 29. The glory of God seen in the storm

1 O give the Lord, you children of God,
give the Lord glory and power;
2 give the Lord the glory of his name.
Adore the Lord in his holy court.

3 The Lord's voice resounding on the waters,
the Lord on the immensity of waters;
4 the voice of the Lord, full of power,
the voice of the Lord, full of splendor.

5 The Lord's voice shattering the cedars,
the Lord shatters the cedars of Lebanon;
6 he makes Lebanon leap like a calf
and Sirion like a young wild ox.

7 (The Lord's voice flashes flames of fire.)

8 The Lord's voice shaking the wilderness,
the Lord shakes the wilderness of Kadesh;
9 the Lord's voice rending the oak tree
and stripping the forest bare.

3b The God of glory thunders.
10 In his temple they all cry: "Glory!"
The Lord sat enthroned over the flood;
the Lord sits as king for ever.

11 The Lord will give strength to his people,
the Lord will bless his people with peace.

(29) 30. Thanksgiving for recovery from sickness

2 I will praise you, Lord, you have rescued me
and have not let my enemies rejoice over me.

* * * * *

3 O Lord, I cried to you for help
and you, my God, have healed me.
4 O Lord, you have raised my soul from the dead,
restored me to life from those who sink into
the grave.

5 Sing psalms to the Lord, you who love him,
give thanks to his holy name.
6 His anger lasts a moment; his favor all through
life.
At night there are tears, but joy comes with dawn.

7 I said to myself in my good fortune:
"Nothing will ever disturb me."
8 Your favor had set me on a mountain fastness,
then you hid your face and I was put to
confusion.

9 To you, Lord, I cried,
to my God I made appeal:
10 "What profit would my death be, my going
to the grave?
Can dust give you praise or proclaim your truth?"

11 The Lord listened and had pity.
The Lord came to my help.
12 For me you have changed my mourning
into dancing,
you removed my sackcloth and clothed me
with joy.
13 So my soul sings psalms to you unceasingly.
O Lord my God, I will thank you for ever.

(30) 31. A prayer of trust in God

In you, O Lord, I take refuge.
Let me never be put to shame.
In your justice, set me free,
hear me and speedily rescue me.

Be a rock of refuge for me,
a mighty stronghold to save me,
for you are my rock, my stronghold.
For your name's sake, lead me and guide me.

Release me from the snares they have hidden
for you are my refuge, Lord.
Into your hands I commend my spirit.
It is you who will redeem me, Lord.

O God of truth, 7 you detest
those who worship false and empty gods.
As for me, I trust in the Lord;
let me be glad and rejoice in your love.

You who have seen my affliction
and taken heed of my soul's distress,
9 have not handed me over to the enemy,
but set my feet at large.

* * * * *

10 Have mercy on me, O Lord,
for I am in distress.
Tears have wasted my eyes,
my throat and my heart.

11 For my life is spent with sorrow
and my years with sighs.
Affliction has broken down my strength
and my bones waste away.

12 In the face of all my foes
I am a reproach,
an object of scorn to my neighbors
and of fear to my friends.

Those who see me in the street
run far away from me.
13 I am like the dead, forgotten by all,
like a thing thrown away.

14 I have heard the slander of the crowd,
fear is all around me,
as they plot together against me,
as they plan to take my life.

15 But as for me, I trust in you, Lord;
I say: "You are my God.
16 My life is in your hands, deliver me
from the hands of those who hate me.

17 Let your face shine on your servant.
Save me in your love.
18 Let me not be put to shame for I call you,
let the wicked be shamed!

Let them be silenced in the grave,
19 let lying lips be mute,
that speak haughtily against the just
with pride and contempt."

* * * * *

20 How great is the goodness, Lord,
that you keep for those who fear you,
that you show to those who trust you
in the sight of all.

21 You hide them in the shelter of your presence
from human plots;
you keep them safe within your tent
from disputing tongues.

22 Blessed be the Lord who has shown me
the wonders of his love
in a fortified city.

23 "I am far removed from your sight"
I said in my alarm.
Yet you heard the voice of my plea
when I cried for help.

24 Love the Lord, all you saints.
He guards his faithful
but the Lord will repay to the full
those who act with pride.

25 Be strong, let your heart take courage,
all who hope in the Lord.

(31) 32. The joy of being forgiven

1 Happy those whose offense is forgiven,
whose sin is remitted.
2 O happy those to whom the Lord
imputes no guilt,
in whose spirit is no guile.

3 I kept it secret and my frame was wasted.
I groaned all day long,
4 for night and day your hand
was heavy upon me.
Indeed my strength was dried up
as by the summer's heat.

5 But now I have acknowledged my sins;
my guilt I did not hide.
I said: "I will confess
my offense to the Lord."
And you, Lord, have forgiven
the guilt of my sin.

6 So let faithful men and women pray to you
in the time of need.
The floods of water may reach high
but they shall stand secure.
7 You are my hiding place, O Lord;
you save me from distress.
(You surround me with cries of deliverance.)

* * * * *

8 I will instruct you and teach you
the way you should go;
I will give you counsel
with my eye upon you.

9 Be not like horse and mule, unintelligent,
needing bridle and bit,
else they will not approach you.
10 Many sorrows has the wicked
but those who trust in the Lord,
loving mercy surrounds them.

* * * * *

11 Rejoice, rejoice in the Lord,
exult, you just!
O come, ring out your joy,
all you upright of heart.

(32) 33. Praise of God's providence

1 Ring out your joy to the Lord, O you just;
for praise is fitting for loyal hearts.

2 Give thanks to the Lord upon the harp,
with a ten-stringed lute sing him songs.
3 O sing him a song that is new,
play loudly, with all your skill.

4 For the word of the Lord is faithful
and all his works to be trusted.
5 The Lord loves justice and right
and fills the earth with his love.

6 By his word the heavens were made,
by the breath of his mouth all the stars.
7 He collects the waves of the ocean;
he stores up the depths of the sea.

8 Let all the earth fear the Lord
all who live in the world revere him.
9 He spoke; and it came to be.
He commanded; it sprang into being.

10 He frustrates the designs of the nations,
he defeats the plans of the peoples.
11 His own designs shall stand for ever,
the plans of his heart from age to age.

12 They are happy, whose God is the Lord,
the people he has chosen as his own.
13 From the heavens the Lord looks forth,
he sees all the peoples of the earth.

14 From the place where he dwells he gazes
on all the dwellers on the earth;
15 he who shapes the hearts of them all
and considers all their deeds.

16 A king is not saved by his army,
nor a warrior preserved by his strength.
17 A vain hope for safety is the horse;
despite its power it cannot save.

18 The Lord looks on those who revere him,
on those who hope in his love,
19 to rescue their souls from death,
to keep them alive in famine.

20 Our soul is waiting for the Lord.
The Lord is our help and our shield.
21 In him do our hearts find joy.
We trust in his holy name.

22 May your love be upon us, O Lord,
as we place all our hope in you.

(33) 34. In praise of God's goodness

2 I will bless the Lord at all times,
his praise always on my lips;
3 in the Lord my soul shall make its boast.
The humble shall hear and be glad.

4 Glorify the Lord with me.
Together let us praise his name.
5 I sought the Lord and he answered me;
from all my terrors he set me free.

6 Look towards him and be radiant;
let your faces not be abashed.
7 When the poor cry out the Lord hears them
and rescues them from all their distress.

8 The angel of the Lord is encamped
around those who revere him, to rescue them.
9 Taste and see that the Lord is good.
They are happy who seek refuge in him.

10 Revere the Lord, you his saints.
They lack nothing, those who revere him.
11 Strong lions suffer want and go hungry
but those who seek the Lord lack no blessing.

12 Come, children, and hear me
that I may teach you the fear of the Lord.
13 Who are those who long for life
and many days, to enjoy their prosperity?

14 Then keep your tongue from evil
and your lips from speaking deceit.
15 Turn aside from evil and do good;
seek and strive after peace.

16 The Lord turns his face against the wicked
to destroy their remembrance from the earth.
17 The Lord turns his eyes to the just
and his ears to their appeal.

18 They call and the Lord hears
and rescues them in all their distress.
19 The Lord is close to the broken-hearted;
those whose spirit is crushed he will save.

20 Many are the trials of the upright
but the Lord will come to rescue them.
21 He will keep guard over all their bones,
not one of their bones shall be broken.

22 Evil brings death to the wicked;
those who hate the good are doomed.
23 The Lord ransoms the souls of his servants.
Those who hide in him shall not be condemned.

(34) 35. An appeal for vindication

1 O Lord, plead my cause against my foes;
fight those who fight me.
2 Take up your buckler and shield;
arise to help me.

3 Take up the javelin and the spear
against those who pursue me.
O Lord, say to my soul:
"I am your salvation."

4 Let those who seek my life
be shamed and disgraced.
Let those who plan evil against me
be routed in confusion.

5 Let them be like chaff before the wind;
let God's angel scatter them.
6 Let their path be slippery and dark;
let God's angel pursue them.

7 They have hidden a net for me wantonly;
they have dug a pit.
8 Let ruin fall upon them
and take them by surprise.
Let them be caught in the net they have hidden;
let them fall into their pit.

9 But my soul shall be joyful in the Lord
and rejoice in his salvation.
10 My whole being will say:
"Lord, who is like you
who rescue the weak from the strong
and the poor from the oppressor?"

11 Lying witnesses arise
and accuse me unjustly.
12 They repay me evil for good;
my soul is forlorn.

13 When they were sick I went into mourning,
afflicted with fasting.
My prayer was ever on my lips,
14 as for a brother, a friend.
I went as though mourning a mother,
bowed down with grief.

15 Now that I am in trouble they gather,
they gather and mock me.
They take me by surprise and strike me
and tear me to pieces.
16 They provoke me with mockery on mockery
and gnash their teeth.

17 O Lord, how long will you look on?
Come to my rescue!
Save my life from these raging beasts,
my soul from these lions.
18 I will thank you in the great assembly,
amid the throng I will praise you.

19 Do not let my lying foes
rejoice over me.
Do not let those who hate me unjustly
wink eyes at each other.

20 They wish no peace to the peaceful
who live in the land.
They make deceitful plots
21 and with mouths wide open
their cry against me is: "Yes!
We saw you do it!"

22 O Lord, you have seen, do not be silent,
do not stand afar off!
23 Awake, stir to my defense,
to my cause, O God!

24 Vindicate me, Lord, in your justice,
do not let them rejoice.
25 Do not let them think: "Yes, we have won,
we have brought you to an end!"

26 Let them be shamed and brought to disgrace
who rejoice at my misfortune.
Let them be covered with shame and confusion
who raise themselves against me.

27 Let there be joy for those who love my cause.
Let them say without end:
"Great is the Lord who delights
in the peace of his servant."
28 Then my tongue shall speak of your justice,
and all day long of your praise.

(35) 36. God's goodness: human malice

2 Sin whispers to sinners
in the depths of their hearts.
There is no fear of God
before their eyes.

3 They so flatter themselves in their minds
that they know not their guilt.
4 In their mouths are mischief and deceit.
All wisdom is gone.

5 They plot the defeat of goodness
as they lie in bed.
They have set their feet on evil ways,
they cling to what is evil.

* * * * *

6 Your love, Lord, reaches to heaven,
your truth to the skies.
7 Your justice is like God's mountain,
your judgments like the deep.

To mortals and beasts you give protection.
O Lord, 8 how precious is your love.
My God, the children of the earth
find refuge in the shelter of your wings.

9 They feast on the riches of your house;
they drink from the stream of your delight.
10 In you is the source of life
and in your light we see light.

11 Keep on loving those who know you,
doing justice for upright hearts.
12 Let the foot of the proud not crush me
nor the hand of the wicked cast me out.

13 See how the evildoers fall!
Flung down, they shall never arise.

(36) 37. Reflections on good and evil

1 Do not fret because of the wicked;
do not envy those who do evil,
2 for they wither quickly like grass
and fade like the green of the fields.

3 If you trust in the Lord and do good,
then you will live in the land and be secure.
4 If you find your delight in the Lord,
he will grant your heart's desire.

5 Commit your life to the Lord,
trust in him and he will act,
6 so that your justice breaks forth like the light,
your cause like the noonday sun.

7 Be still before the Lord and wait in patience;
do not fret at those who prosper;
those who make evil plots
14c to bring down the needy and the poor.

8 Calm your anger and forget your rage;
do not fret, it only leads to evil.
9 For those who do evil shall perish;
the patient shall inherit the land.

10 A little longer — and the wicked shall have gone.
Look at their homes, they are not there.
11 But the humble shall own the land
and enjoy the fullness of peace.

12 The wicked make plots against the just
and gnash their teeth against them;
13 but the Lord laughs at the wicked
for he sees that their day is at hand.

14 The sword of the wicked is drawn,
the bow bent to slaughter the upright.
15 Their sword shall pierce their own hearts
and their bows shall be broken to pieces.

16 The few things owned by the just
are better than the wealth of the wicked;
17 for the power of the wicked shall be broken
and the Lord will support the just.

18 He protects the lives of the upright,
their heritage will last for ever.
19 They shall not be put to shame in evil days,
in time of famine their food shall not fail.

20 But all the wicked shall perish
and all the enemies of the Lord.
They are like the beauty of the meadows,
they shall vanish, they shall vanish like smoke.

21 The wicked borrow without repaying,
but the just are generous and give.
22 Those blessed by the Lord shall own the land,
but those he has cursed shall be destroyed.

23 The Lord guards the steps of the upright
and makes safe the path of those he loves.
24 Though they stumble they shall never fall
for the Lord holds them by the hand.

25 I was young and now I am old,
but I have never seen the just forsaken
nor their children begging for bread.
26 All the day they are generous and lend
and their children become a blessing.

27 Then turn away from evil and do good
and you shall have a home for ever;
28 for the Lord loves justice
and will never forsake his friends.

The unjust shall be wiped out for ever
and the children of the wicked destroyed.
29 The just shall inherit the land;
there they shall live for ever.

30 The mouths of the just speak wisdom
and their lips say what is right;
31 the law of their God is in their heart,
their steps shall be saved from stumbling.

32 The wicked are watching for the just
and seeking occasion to destroy them.
33 The Lord will not leave them undefended
nor let them be condemned when they
are judged.

34 Then wait for the Lord, keep to his way.
It is he who will free you from the wicked,
raise you up to possess the land
and see the wicked destroyed.

35 I have seen the wicked triumphant,
towering like the cedars of Lebanon.
36 I passed by again; they were gone.
I searched; they could not be found.

37 See the just, and mark the upright,
a future lies in store for the peaceful,
38 but sinners shall all be destroyed.
No future lies in store for the wicked.

39 The salvation of the just comes from the Lord,
their stronghold in time of distress.
40 The Lord helps them and delivers them
and saves them, for their refuge is in him.

(37) 38. Acknowledgment of guilt

2 O Lord, do not rebuke me in your anger;
do not punish me, Lord, in your rage.
3 Your arrows have sunk deep in me;

your hand has come down upon me.
4 Through your anger all my body is sick;
through my sin, there is no health in my limbs.

5 My guilt towers higher than my head;
it is a weight too heavy to bear.
6 My wounds are foul and festering,
the result of my own folly.
7 I am bowed and brought to my knees.
I go mourning all the day long.

8 All my frame burns with fever;
all my body is sick.
9 Spent and utterly crushed,
I cry aloud in anguish of heart.

10 O Lord, you know all my longing;
my groans are not hidden from you.
11 My heart throbs, my strength is spent;
the very light has gone from my eyes.

12 My friends avoid me like a leper;
those closest to me stand afar off.
13 Those who plot against my life lay snares;
those who seek my ruin speak of harm,
planning treachery all the day long.

14 But I am like the deaf who cannot hear,
like the mute I cannot open my mouth.
15 I am like one who hears nothing
in whose mouth is no defense.

16 I count on you, O Lord;
it is you, Lord God, who will answer.
17 I pray: "Do not let them mock me,
those who triumph if my foot should slip."

18 For I am on the point of falling
and my pain is always before me.
19 I confess that I am guilty
and my sin fills me with dismay.

20 My wanton enemies are numberless
and my lying foes are many.
21 They repay me evil for good
and attack me for seeking what is right.

22 O Lord, do not forsake me!
My God, do not stay afar off!
23 Make haste and come to my help,
O Lord, my God, my savior!

(38) 39. No abiding city

2 I said: "I will be watchful of my ways
for fear I should sin with my tongue.
I will put a curb on my lips
when the wicked stand before me."
3 I was mute, silent and still.
Their prosperity stirred my grief.

4 My heart was burning within me.
At the thought of it, the fire blazed up
and my tongue burst into speech:
5 "O Lord, you have shown me my end,
how short is the length of my days.
Now I know how fleeting is my life.

6 You have given me a short span of days;
my life is as nothing in your sight.
A mere breath, the one who stood so firm;

7 a mere shadow, the one who passes by;
a mere breath, the hoarded riches,
and who will take them, no one knows."

8 And now, Lord, what is there to wait for?
In you rests all my hope.
9 Set me free from all my sins;
do not make me the taunt of the fool.
10 I was silent, not opening my lips,
because this was all your doing.

11 Take away your scourge from me.
I am crushed by the blows of your hand.
12 You punish our sins and correct us;
like a moth you devour all we treasure.
Human life is no more than a breath;
13 O Lord, hear my prayer.

O Lord, turn your ear to my cry.
Do not be deaf to my tears.
In your house I am a passing guest,
a pilgrim, like all my forebears.
14 Look away that I may breathe again
before I depart to be no more.

(39) 40. A song of praise

2 I waited, I waited for the Lord
and he stooped down to me;
he heard my cry.

3 He drew me from the deadly pit,
from the miry clay.
He set my feet upon a rock
and made my footsteps firm.

4 He put a new song into my mouth,
praise of our God.
Many shall see and fear
and shall trust in the Lord.

5 Happy those who have placed
their trust in the Lord
and have not gone over to the rebels
who follow false gods.

6 How many, O Lord my God,
are the wonders and designs
that you have worked for us;
you have no equal.
Should I proclaim and speak of them,
they are more than I can tell!

7 You do not ask for sacrifice and offerings,
but an open ear.
You do not ask for holocaust and victim.
8 Instead, here am I.

In the scroll of the book it stands written
9 that I should do your will.
My God, I delight in your law
in the depth of my heart.

10 Your justice I have proclaimed
in the great assembly.
My lips I have not sealed;
you know it, O Lord.

11 I have not hidden your justice in my heart
but declared your faithful help.
I have not hidden your love and your truth
from the great assembly.

12 O Lord, you will not withhold
your compassion from me.
Your merciful love and your truth
will always guard me.

13 For I am beset with evils
too many to be counted.
My sins have fallen upon me
and my sight fails me.
They are more than the hairs of my head
and my heart sinks.

14 O Lord, come to my rescue;
Lord, come to my aid.
15 O let there be shame and confusion
on those who seek my life.

O let them turn back in confusion,
who delight in my harm.
16 Let them be appalled, covered with shame,
who jeer at my lot.

17 O let there be rejoicing and gladness
for all who seek you.
Let them ever say: "The Lord is great",
who love your saving help.

18 As for me, wretched and poor,
the Lord thinks of me.
You are my rescuer, my help,
O God, do not delay.

(40) 41. Prayer in sickness and betrayal

2 Happy those who consider the poor and
the weak.
The Lord will save them in the evil day,
3 will guard them, give them life, make them
happy in the land
and will not give them up to the will of their foes.
4 The Lord will give them strength in their pain,
will bring them back from sickness to health.

5 As for me, I said: "Lord, have mercy on me,
heal my soul for I have sinned against you."
6 My foes are speaking evil against me.
They want me to die and my name to perish.
7 They come to visit me and speak empty words,
their hearts full of malice, they spread it abroad.

8 My enemies whisper together against me.
They all weigh up the evil which is on me.
They say something deadly is fixed upon me
and I will not rise from where I lie.
10 Thus even my friend, in whom I trusted,
who ate my bread, has turned against me.

11 But you, O Lord, have mercy on me.
Let me rise once more and I will repay them.
12 By this I shall know that you are my friend,
if my foes do not shout in triumph over me.
13 If you uphold me I shall be unharmed
and set in your presence for evermore.

* * * * *

14 Blessed be the Lord, the God of Israel
from age to age. Amen. Amen.

(41) 42. The prayer of an exile

2 Like the deer that yearns
for running streams,
so my soul is yearning
for you, my God.

3 My soul is thirsting for God,
the God of my life;
when can I enter and see
the face of God?

4 My tears have become my bread,
by night, by day,
as I hear it said all the day long:
"Where is your God?"

5 These things will I remember
as I pour out my soul:
how I would lead the rejoicing crowd
into the house of God,
amid cries of gladness and thanksgiving,
the throng wild with joy.

6 Why are you cast down, my soul,
why groan within me?
Hope in God; I will praise him still,
my savior and my God.

7 My soul is cast down within me
as I think of you,
from the country of Jordan and Mount Hermon,
from the Hill of Mizar.

8 Deep is calling on deep,
in the roar of waters;
your torrents and all your waves
swept over me.

9 By day the Lord will send
his loving kindness;
by night I will sing to him,
praise the God of my life.

10 I will say to God, my rock:
"Why have you forgotten me?
Why do I go mourning
oppressed by the foe?"

11 With cries that pierce me to the heart,
my enemies revile me,
saying to me all the day long:
"Where is your God?"

12 Why are you cast down, my soul,
why groan within me?
Hope in God; I will praise him still,
my savior and my God.

(42) 43. Longing for God's dwelling place

1 Defend me, O God, and plead my cause
against a godless nation.
From a deceitful and cunning people
rescue me, O God.

2 Since you, O God, are my stronghold,
why have you rejected me?
Why do I go mourning
oppressed by the foe?

3 O send forth your light and your truth;
let these be my guide.
Let them bring me to your holy mountain,
to the place where you dwell.

4 And I will come to your altar, O God,
the God of my joy.
My redeemer, I will thank you on the harp,
O God, my God.

5 Why are you cast down, my soul,
why groan within me?
Hope in God; I will praise him still,
my savior and my God.

(43) 44. A lament in time of calamity

2 We heard with our own ears, O God,
our forebears have told us the story
of the things you did in their days,
you yourself, in days long ago.

3 To plant them you uprooted the nations;
to let them spread you laid peoples low.
4 No sword of their own won the land;
no arm of their own brought them victory.
It was your right hand, your arm
and the light of your face; for you loved them.

5 It is you, my king, my God,
who granted victories to Jacob.
6 Through you we beat down our foes;
in your name we trampled our aggressors.

7 For it was not in my bow that I trusted
nor yet was I saved by my sword;
8 it was you who saved us from our foes,
it was you who put our foes to shame.
9 All day long our boast was in God
and we praised your name without ceasing.

10 Yet now you have rejected us, disgraced us;
you no longer go forth with our armies.
11 You make us retreat from the foe
and our enemies plunder us at will.

12 You make us like sheep for the slaughter
and scatter us among the nations.
13 You sell your own people for nothing
and make no profit by the sale.

14 You make us the taunt of our neighbors,
the laughing stock of all who are near.
15 Among the nations, you make us a byword,
among the peoples a thing of derision.

16 All day long my disgrace is before me;
my face is covered with shame
17 at the voice of the taunter, the scoffer,
at the sight of the foe and avenger.

* * * * *

18 This befell us though we had not forgotten you,
though we had not been false to your covenant,
19 though we had not withdrawn our hearts,
though our feet had not strayed from your path.
20 Yet you have crushed us in a place of sorrows
and covered us with the shadow of death.

21 Had we forgotten your name, O God,
or stretched out our hands to another god,
22 would you not have found this out,
you who know the secrets of the heart?
23 It is for you we face death all day long
and are counted as sheep for the slaughter.

24 Awake, O Lord, why do you sleep?
Arise, do not reject us for ever!
25 Why do you hide your face
and forget our oppression and misery?

26 For we are brought down low to the dust;
our body lies prostrate on the earth.
27 Stand up and come to our help!
Redeem us because of your love!

(44) 45. Royal wedding song

2 My heart overflows with noble words.
To the king I must speak the song I have made,
my tongue as nimble as the pen of a scribe.

3 You are the fairest of the people on earth
and graciousness is poured upon your lips,
because God has blessed you for evermore.

4 O mighty one, gird your sword upon your thigh;
in splendor and state, 5 ride on in triumph
for the cause of truth and goodness and right.

Take aim with your bow in your dread right hand.
6 Your arrows are sharp, peoples fall beneath you.
The foes of the king fall down and lose heart.

7 Your throne, O God, shall endure for ever.
A scepter of justice is the scepter of your kingdom.
8 Your love is for justice, your hatred for evil.

Therefore God, your God, has anointed you
with the oil of gladness above other kings;
9 your robes are fragrant with aloes and myrrh.

From the ivory palace you are greeted with music.
10 The daughters of kings are among your loved ones.
On your right stands the queen in gold of Ophir.

* * * * *

11 Listen, O daughter, give ear to my words:
forget your own people and your father's house.
12 So will the king desire your beauty;
he is your lord, pay homage to him.

13 And the people of Tyre shall come with gifts,
the richest of the people shall seek your favor.
14 The daughter of the king is clothed with splendor,
her robes embroidered with pearls set in gold.

15 She is led to the king with her maiden companions.
16 They are escorted amid gladness and joy;
they pass within the palace of the king.

* * * * *

17 Children shall be yours in place of your forebears;
you will make them rulers over all the earth.

18 May this song make your name for ever
remembered.
May the peoples praise you from age to age.

(45) 46. God is with us

2 God is for us a refuge and strength,
a helper close at hand, in time of distress,
3 so we shall not fear though the earth should rock,
though the mountains fall into the depths of
the sea;
4 even though its waters rage and foam,
even though the mountains be shaken by its
waves.

The Lord of hosts is with us;
the God of Jacob is our stronghold.

5 The waters of a river give joy to God's city,
the holy place where the Most High dwells.
6 God is within, it cannot be shaken;
God will help it at the dawning of the day.
7 Nations are in tumult, kingdoms are shaken;
he lifts his voice, the earth shrinks away.

8 The Lord of hosts is with us;
the God of Jacob is our stronghold.

9 Come, consider the works of the Lord,
the redoubtable deeds he has done on the earth.
10 He puts an end to wars over all the earth;
the bow he breaks, the spear he snaps.
(He burns the shields with fire.)
11 "Be still and know that I am God,
supreme among the nations, supreme on
the earth!"

12 The Lord of hosts is with us;
the God of Jacob is our stronghold.

(46) 47. God, king of the world

2 All peoples, clap your hands,
cry to God with shouts of joy!
3 For the Lord, the Most High, we must fear,
great king over all the earth.

4 He subdues peoples under us
and nations under our feet.
5 Our inheritance, our glory, is from him,
given to Jacob out of love.

6 God goes up with shouts of joy;
the Lord goes up with trumpet blast.
7 Sing praise for God, sing praise,
sing praise to our king, sing praise.

8 God is king of all the earth,
sing praise with all your skill.
9 God is king over the nations;
God reigns on his holy throne.

10 The leaders of the people are assembled
with the people of Abraham's God.
The rulers of the earth belong to God,
to God who reigns over all.

(47) 48. The invincible city of God

2 The Lord is great and worthy to be praised
in the city of our God.

His holy mountain [3] rises in beauty,
the joy of all the earth.

Mount Zion, true pole of the earth,
the Great King's city!
4 God, in the midst of its citadels,
has shown himself its stronghold.

5 For the kings assembled together,
together they advanced.
6 They saw; at once they were astounded;
dismayed, they fled in fear.

7 A trembling seized them there,
like the pangs of birth.
8 By the east wind you have destroyed
the ships of Tarshish.

9 As we have heard, so we have seen
in the city of our God,
in the city of the Lord of hosts
which God upholds for ever.

10 O God, we ponder your love
within your temple.
11 Your praise, O God, like your name
reaches the ends of the earth.

With justice your right hand is filled.
12 Mount Zion rejoices;
the people of Judah rejoice
at the sight of your judgments.

13 Walk through Zion, walk all round it;
count the number of its towers.
14 Review all its ramparts,
examine its castles,

that you may tell the next generation
15 that such is our God,
our God for ever and always.
It is he who leads us.

(48) 49. The problem of justice and death

2 Hear this, all you peoples,
give heed, all who dwell in the world,
3 people high and low,
rich and poor alike!

4 My lips will speak words of wisdom.
My heart is full of insight.
5 I will turn my mind to a parable,
with the harp I will solve my problem.

* * * * *

6 Why should I fear in evil days
the malice of the foes who surround me,
7 people who trust in their wealth,
and boast of the vastness of their riches?

8 For the rich cannot buy their own ransom,
nor pay a price to God for their lives.
9 The ransom of their souls is beyond them.
10 They cannot buy life without end,
nor avoid coming to the grave.

11 They know that both wise and foolish perish
and must leave their wealth to others.
12 Their graves are their homes for ever,
their dwelling place from age to age,
though their names spread wide through
the land.

13 In their riches, people lack wisdom;
they are like the beasts that are destroyed.

* * * * *

14 This is the lot of those who trust in themselves,
who have others at their beck and call.
15 Like sheep they are driven to the grave,
where death shall be their shepherd
and the just shall become their rulers.

With the morning their outward show vanishes
and the grave becomes their home.
16 But God will ransom me from death
and take my soul to himself.

17 Then do not fear when others grow rich,
when the glory of their house increases.
18 They take nothing with them when they die,
their glory does not follow them below.

19 Though they flattered themselves while they
lived:
"They will praise me for doing well for myself,"
20 yet they will go to join their forebears,
and will never see the light any more.

21 In their riches, people lack wisdom;
they are like the beasts that are destroyed.

(49) 50. True worship

1 The God of gods, the Lord,
has spoken and summoned the earth,
from the rising of the sun to its setting.
2 Out of Zion's perfect beauty he shines.

3 (Our God comes, he keeps silence no longer.)

Before him fire devours,
around him tempest rages.
4 He calls on the heavens and the earth
to witness his judgment of his people.

5 "Summon before me my people
who made covenant with me by sacrifice."
6 The heavens proclaim his justice,
for he, God, is the judge.

7 "Listen, my people, I will speak;
Israel, I will testify against you,
for I am God, your God.
21c I accuse you, lay the charge before you.

8 I find no fault with your sacrifices,
your offerings are always before me.
9 I do not ask more bullocks from your farms,
nor goats from among your herds.

10 For I own all the beasts of the forest,
beasts in their thousands on my hills.
11 I know all the birds in the sky,
all that moves in the field belongs to me.

12 Were I hungry, I would not tell you,
for I own the world and all it holds.
13 Do you think I eat the flesh of bulls,
or drink the blood of goats?

14 Pay your sacrifice of thanksgiving to God
and render him your votive offerings.
15 Call on me in the day of distress.
I will free you and you shall honor me."

16 (But God says to the wicked:)

"But how can you recite my commandments
and take my covenant on your lips,
17 you who despise my law
and throw my words to the winds,

18 you who see thieves and go with them;
who throw in your lot with adulterers,
19 who unbridle your mouth for evil
and whose tongue is plotting crime,

20 you who sit and malign your kinsfolk
and slander your brothers and sisters.
21 You do this, and should I keep silence?
Do you think that I am like you?

22 Mark this, you who never think of God,
lest I seize you and you cannot escape;
23 a sacrifice of thanksgiving honors me
and I will show God's salvation to the upright."

(50) 51. A prayer of contrition: fourth psalm of repentance

3 Have mercy on me, God, in your kindness.
In your compassion blot out my offense.
4 O wash me more and more from my guilt
and cleanse me from my sin.

5 My offenses truly I know them;
my sin is always before me.
6 Against you, you alone, have I sinned;
what is evil in your sight I have done.

That you may be justified when you give sentence
and be without reproach when you judge,
7 O see, in guilt I was born,
a sinner was I conceived.

8 Indeed you love truth in the heart;
then in the secret of my heart teach me wisdom.
9 O purify me, then I shall be clean;
O wash me, I shall be whiter than snow.

10 Make me hear rejoicing and gladness
that the bones you have crushed may thrill.
11 From my sins turn away your face
and blot out all my guilt.

12 A pure heart create for me, O God,
put a steadfast spirit within me.
13 Do not cast me away from your presence,
nor deprive me of your holy spirit.

14 Give me again the joy of your help;
with a spirit of fervor sustain me,
15 that I may teach transgressors your ways
and sinners may return to you.

16 O rescue me, God, my helper,
and my tongue shall ring out your goodness.
17 O Lord, open my lips
and my mouth shall declare your praise.

18 For in sacrifice you take no delight,
burnt offering from me you would refuse;
19 my sacrifice, a contrite spirit,
a humbled, contrite heart you will not spurn.

20 In your goodness, show favor to Zion;
rebuild the walls of Jerusalem.
21 Then you will be pleased with lawful sacrifice,
(burnt offerings wholly consumed),
then you will be offered young bulls on your altar.

(51) 52. The fate of the deceitful

3 Why do you boast of your wickedness,
you champion of evil,
4 planning ruin all day long,
(your tongue like a sharpened razor),
you dealer in deceit?

5 You love evil more than good,
lies more than truth.
6 You love the destructive word,
you tongue of deceit.

7 For this God will destroy you
and remove you for ever.
He will snatch you from your tent and uproot you
from the land of the living.

8 The just shall see and fear.
They shall laugh and say:
9 "So this is the one who refused
to take God as a stronghold,
but trusted in the power of wealth
and grew powerful through crime."

10 But I am like a growing olive tree
in the house of God.
I trust in the goodness of God
for ever and ever.

11 I will thank you for evermore;
for this is your doing.
I will proclaim that your name is good,
in the presence of your friends.

(52) 53. Fools

2 Fools have said in their hearts:
"There is no God above."
Their deeds are corrupt, depraved;
there is no good person left.

3 God looks down from heaven
on the peoples of the earth,
to see if any are wise,
if any seek God.

4 All have left the right path;
depraved, every one.
There is no good person left,
no, not even one.

5 Will the evildoers not understand?
They eat up my people
as though they were eating bread;
they never pray to God.

6 See how they tremble with fear
without cause for fear;
for God scatters the bones of the wicked.
They are shamed, God rejects them.

7 O that Israel's salvation might come from Zion!
When God delivers his people from bondage,
then Jacob will be glad and Israel rejoice.

See psalm (13) 14

(53) 54. A prayer for God's help

3 O God, save me by your name;
by your power, uphold my cause.
4 O God, hear my prayer;
listen to the words of my mouth.

5 For the proud have risen against me,
ruthless foes seek my life.
They have no regard for God.

6 But I have God for my help.
The Lord upholds my life.
7 Let the evil recoil upon my foes;
you who are faithful, destroy them.

8 I will sacrifice to you with willing heart
and praise your name for it is good;
9 for you have rescued me from all my distress
and my eyes have seen the downfall of my foes.

(54) 55. A prayer in betrayal and distress

2 O God, listen to my prayer,
do not hide from my pleading,
3 attend to me and reply;
with my cares, I cannot rest.

I tremble 4 at the shouts of the foe,
at the cries of the wicked;
for they bring down evil upon me.
They assail me with fury.

5 My heart is stricken within me,
death's terror is on me,
6 trembling and fear fall upon me
and horror overwhelms me.

7 O that I had wings like a dove
to fly away and be at rest.
8 So I would escape far away
and take refuge in the desert.

9 I would hasten to find a shelter
from the raging wind,
from the destructive storm, O Lord,
10 and from their plotting tongues.

For I can see nothing but violence
and strife in the city.
11 Night and day they patrol
high on the city walls.

It is full of wickedness and evil,
12 it is full of sin.
Its streets are never free
from tyranny and deceit.

13 If this had been done by an enemy
then I could bear it.
If a rival had risen against me,
then I could hide.

14 But it is you, my own companion,
my intimate friend!
15 (How close was the friendship between us.)
We walked together in harmony
in the house of God.

16 May death fall suddenly upon them!
Let them go to the grave;
for wickedness dwells in their homes
and deep in their hearts.

17 As for me, I will cry to God
and the Lord will save me.
18 Evening, morning and at noon
I will cry and lament.

19 God will deliver my soul in peace
in the attack against me;
for those who fight me are many,
18c but he hears my voice.

20 God will hear and will humble them,
the eternal judge;
for they will not amend their ways.
They have no fear of God.

21 The traitor has turned against me;
has broken our pact,
22 with speech softer than butter,
but war within the heart,
with words smoother than oil,
though they are naked swords.

23 Entrust your cares to the Lord
and he will support you.
He will never allow
the just one to stumble.

24 But you, O God, will bring them down
to the pit of death.
The bloodthirsty and the deceitful
shall not live half their lives.

O Lord, I will trust in you.

(55) 56. Unshakable trust in God

2 Have mercy on me, God, foes crush me;
they fight me all day long and oppress me.
3 My foes crush me all day long,
for many fight proudly against me.

4 When I fear, I will trust in you,
5 in God whose word I praise.
In God I trust, I shall not fear;
what can mere mortals do to me?

6 All day long they distort my words,
all their thought is to harm me.
7 They band together in ambush,
track me down and seek my life.

8 Repay them, God, for their crimes;
in your anger, cast down the peoples.
9 You have kept an account of my wanderings;
you have kept a record of my tears;
(are they not written in your book?)
10 Then my foes will be put to flight
on the day that I call to you.

This I know, that God is on my side.
11 In God, whose word I praise,
(in the Lord, whose word I praise,)
12 in God I trust; I shall not fear;
what can mere mortals do to me?

13 I am bound by the vows I have made you.
O God, I will offer you praise
14 for you rescued my soul from death,
you kept my feet from stumbling
that I may walk in the presence of God
and enjoy the light of the living.

(56) 57. In time of danger

2 Have mercy on me, God, have mercy
for in you my soul has taken refuge.
In the shadow of your wings I take refuge
till the storms of destruction pass by.

3 I call to you God the Most High,
to you who have always been my help.
4 May you send from heaven and save me
and shame those who assail me.

O God, send your truth and your love.

5 My soul lies down among lions,
who would devour us, one and all.
Their teeth are spears and arrows,
their tongue a sharpened sword.

6 O God, arise above the heavens;
may your glory shine on earth!

7 They laid a snare for my steps
my soul was bowed down.
They dug a pit in my path
but fell in it themselves.

8 My heart is ready, O God,
my heart is ready.
I will sing, I will sing your praise.
9 Awake, my soul;
awake, lyre and harp,
I will awake the dawn.

10 I will thank you, Lord, among the peoples,
among the nations I will praise you
11 for your love reaches to the heavens
and your truth to the skies.

12 O God, arise above the heavens;
may your glory shine on earth!

(57) 58. Condemnation of injustice

2 Do you truly speak justice, you who hold
divine power?
Do you mete out fair judgment to the people
of the land?
3 No, in your hearts you devise injustice;
your hands deal out violence to the land.

4 In their wickedness they have gone astray
from their birth;
they wandered among lies as soon as they
were born.
5 Their venom is like the venom of the snake;
they are heedless as the adder that turns a
deaf ear
6 lest it should catch the snake charmer's voice,
the voice of the skillful dealer in spells.

7 O God, break the teeth in their mouths,
tear out the fangs of these wild beasts, O Lord!
8 Let them vanish like water that runs away;
let them wither like grass that is trodden
underfoot;
9 let them be like the snail that dissolves into slime;
like a woman's miscarriage that never sees
the sun.

10 Before they put forth thorns, like a bramble,
let them be swept away, green wood or dry!
11 The just shall rejoice at the sight of vengeance;
they shall bathe their feet in the blood of
the wicked.
12 "Truly", all shall say, "the just are rewarded.
Truly there is a God who does justice on
the earth."

(58) 59. A prayer for safety

2 Rescue me, God, from my foes;
protect me from those who attack me.
3 O rescue me from those who do evil
and save me from bloodthirsty enemies.

4 See, they lie in wait for my life;
the powerful band together against me.
For no offense, no sin of mine, Lord,
5 for no guilt of mine they rush to take their stand.

Awake, come to my aid and see!
6 Lord of hosts, you are Israel's God.
Rouse yourself and punish the nations;
show no mercy to evil traitors.

7 Each evening they come back like dogs.
They howl and roam about the city;
they prowl in search of food;
they snarl till they have their fill.

8 See how they gabble open-mouthed;
their lips are filled with insults.
"For who," they say, "will hear us?"
9 But you, Lord, will laugh them to scorn.
You make light of all the nations.

10 O my Strength, it is you to whom I turn,
for you, O God, are my stronghold,
11 the God who shows me love.

O God, come to my aid
and let me look in triumph on my foes.
12 God, kill them lest my people be seduced;
rout them by your power, lay them low.

It is you, O Lord, who are our shield.
13 For the sins of their mouths and their lips,
for the curses and lies that they speak
let them be caught in their pride.

14 Destroy them, Lord, in your anger.
Destroy them till they are no more.
Let the world know that you are the ruler
over Jacob and the ends of the earth.

5 Each evening they come back like dogs.
They howl and roam about the city;
6 they prowl in search of food;
they snarl till they have their fill.

17 As for me, I will sing of your strength
and each morning acclaim your love
for you have been my stronghold,
a refuge in the day of my distress.

18 O my Strength, it is you to whom I turn,
for you, O God, are my stronghold,
the God who shows me love.

(59) 60. After a defeat in battle

3 O God, you have rejected us and broken us.
You have been angry; come back to us.

4 You have made the earth quake, torn it open.
Repair what is shattered for it sways.
5 You have inflicted hardships on your people
and made us drink a wine that dazed us.

6 You have given those who fear you a signal
to flee from the enemy's bow.
7 O come, and deliver your friends,
help with your right hand and reply.

* * * * *

8 From his holy place God has made this promise;
"I will triumph and divide the land of Shechem,
I will measure out the valley of Succoth.

9 Gilead is mine and Manasseh,
Ephraim I take for my helmet,
Judah for my commander's staff.

10 Moab I will use for my washbowl;
on Edom I will plant my shoe.
Over the Philistines I will shout in triumph."

11 But who will lead me to conquer the fortress?
Who will bring me face to face with Edom?
12 Will you utterly reject us, O God,
and no longer march with our armies?

13 Give us help against the foe,
for human help is vain.
14 With God we shall do bravely
and he will trample down our foes.

See psalm (107) 108

(60) 61. Prayer of an exile

2 O God, hear my cry!
Listen to my prayer!
3 From the end of the earth I call;
my heart is faint.

On a rock too high for me to reach
set me on high,
O you who have been my refuge,
my tower against the foe.

Let me dwell in your tent for ever
and hide in the shelter of your wings.
For you, O God, hear my prayer,
grant me the heritage of those who fear you.

May you lengthen the life of the king;
may his years cover many generations.
May he ever sit enthroned before God;
bid love and truth be his protection.

9 So I will always praise your name
and day after day fulfill my vows.

(61) 62. God, the rock of strength

2 In God alone is my soul at rest;
my help comes from him.
3 He alone is my rock, my stronghold,
my fortress; I stand firm.

4 How long will you attack me
to break me down,
as though I were a tottering wall,
or a tumbling fence?

5 Their plan is only to destroy;
they take pleasure in lies.
With their mouth they utter blessing
but in their heart they curse.

6 In God alone be at rest, my soul;
for my hope comes from him.
7 He alone is my rock, my stronghold,
my fortress; I stand firm.

8 In God is my safety and glory,
the rock of my strength.
Take refuge in God, 9 all you people.
Trust him at all times.
Pour out your hearts before him
for God is our refuge.

10 Common folk are only a breath,
the great are an illusion.
Placed in the scales, they rise;
they weigh less than a breath.

11 Do not put your trust in oppression
nor vain hopes on plunder.
Do not set your heart on riches
even when they increase.

12 For God has said only one thing;
only two do I know:
that to God alone belongs power
13 and to you, Lord, love;
and that you repay us all
according to our deeds.

(62) 63. Longing for God

O God, you are my God, for you I long;
for you my soul is thirsting.
My body pines for you
like a dry, weary land without water.
So I gaze on you in the sanctuary
to see your strength and your glory.

For your love is better than life,
my lips will speak your praise.
So I will bless you all my life,
in your name I will lift up my hands.
My soul shall be filled as with a banquet,
my mouth shall praise you with joy.

On my bed I remember you.
On you I muse through the night
for you have been my help;
in the shadow of your wings I rejoice.
My soul clings to you;
your right hand holds me fast.

10 Those who seek to destroy my life
shall go down to the depths of the earth.
11 They shall be put into the power of the sword
and left as the prey of the jackals.
12 But the king shall rejoice in God;
(all that swear by him shall be blessed,)
for the mouth of liars shall be silenced.

(63) 64. A prayer for God's protection

2 Hear my voice, O God, as I complain,
guard my life from dread of the foe.
3 Hide me from the band of the wicked,
from the throng of those who do evil.

4 They sharpen their tongues like swords;
they aim bitter words like arrows
5 to shoot at the innocent from ambush,
shooting suddenly and recklessly.

6 They scheme their evil course;
they conspire to lay secret snares.
They say: "Who will see us?
7 Who can search out our crimes?"

* * * * *

He will search who searches the mind
and knows the depths of the heart.
8 God has shot them with his arrow
and dealt them sudden wounds.
9 Their own tongue has brought them to ruin
and all who see them mock.

0 Then all the world will fear;
they will tell what God has done.
They will understand God's deeds.
1 The just will rejoice in the Lord
and fly to him for refuge.
All the upright hearts will glory.

64) 65. A song of springtime

To you our praise is due
in Zion, O God.
To you we pay our vows,
you who hear our prayer.

To you all flesh will come
with its burden of sin.
Too heavy for us, our offences,
but you wipe them away.

Blessed those whom you choose and call
to dwell in your courts.
We are filled with the blessings of your house,
of your holy temple.

You keep your pledge with wonders,
O God our savior,
the hope of all the earth
and of far distant isles.

You uphold the mountains with your strength,
you are girded with power.
You still the roaring of the seas,
(the roaring of their waves,)
and the tumult of the peoples.

9 The ends of the earth stand in awe
at the sight of your wonders.
The lands of sunrise and sunset
you fill with your joy.

10 You care for the earth, give it water;
you fill it with riches.
Your river in heaven brims over
to provide its grain.

And thus you provide for the earth;
11 you drench its furrows;
you level it, soften it with showers;
you bless its growth.

12 You crown the year with your goodness.
Abundance flows in your steps;
13 in the pastures of the wilderness it flows.

The hills are girded with joy,
14 the meadows covered with flocks,
the valleys are decked with wheat.
They shout for joy, yes, they sing.

(65) 66. A people's thanksgiving

1 Cry out with joy to God all the earth,
2 O sing to the glory of his name.
O render him glorious praise.
3 Say to God: "How tremendous your deeds!

Because of the greatness of your strength
your enemies cringe before you.
4 Before you all the earth shall bow,
shall sing to you, sing to your name!"

Come and see the works of God,
tremendous his deeds among the peoples.
He turned the sea into dry land,
they passed through the river dry-shod.

Let our joy then be in him;
he rules for ever by his might.
His eyes keep watch over the nations;
let rebels not rise against him.

O peoples, bless our God;
let the voice of his praise resound,
of the God who gave life to our souls
and kept our feet from stumbling.

For you, O God, have tested us,
you have tried us as silver is tried;
you led us, God, into the snare;
you laid a heavy burden on our backs.

You let foes ride over our heads;
we went through fire and through water
but then you brought us relief.

Burnt offering I bring to your house;
to you I will pay my vows,
the vows which my lips have uttered,
which my mouth spoke in my distress.

I will offer burnt offerings of fatlings
with the smoke of burning rams.
I will offer bullocks and goats.

Come and hear, all who fear God,
I will tell what he did for my soul;
to him I cried aloud,
with high praise ready on my tongue.

18 If there had been evil in my heart,
the Lord would not have listened.
19 But truly God has listened;
he has heeded the voice of my prayer.

20 Blessed be God who did not reject my prayer
nor withhold his love from me.

(66) 67. A harvest song

2 O God, be gracious and bless us
and let your face shed its light upon us.
3 So will your ways be known upon earth
and all nations learn your saving help.

4 Let the peoples praise you, O God;
let all the peoples praise you.

5 Let the nations be glad and exult
for you rule the world with justice.
With fairness you rule the peoples,
you guide the nations on earth.

6 Let the peoples praise you, O God;
let all the peoples praise you.

7 The earth has yielded its fruit
for God, our God, has blessed us.
8 May God still give us his blessing
till the ends of the earth revere him.

Let the peoples praise you, O God;
let all the peoples praise you.

(67) 68. A commemoration of victory

2 Let God arise, let his foes be scattered.
Let those who hate him flee before him.
3 As smoke is blown away so will they be blown away;
like wax that melts before the fire,
so the wicked shall perish at the presence of God.

4 But the just shall rejoice at the presence of God,
they shall exult and dance for joy.
5 O sing to the Lord, make music to his name;
make a highway for him who rides on the clouds.
Rejoice in the Lord, exult at his presence.

6 Father of the orphan, defender of the widow,
such is God in his holy place.
7 God gives the lonely a home to live in;
he leads the prisoners forth into freedom;
but rebels must dwell in a parched land.

8 When you went forth, O God, at the head of your people,
when you marched across the desert, 9 the earth trembled,
the heavens melted at the presence of God,
at the presence of God, Israel's God.

10 You poured down, O God, a generous rain;
when your people were starved you gave them new life.
11 It was there that your people found a home,
prepared in your goodness, O God, for the poor.

12 The Lord gives the word to the bearers of good tidings:
"The Almighty has defeated a numberless army

13 and kings and armies are in flight, in flight
while you were at rest among the sheepfolds."

14 At home the women already share the spoil.
They are covered with silver as the wings of a dove,
its feathers brilliant with shining gold
15 and jewels flashing like snow on Mount Zalmon.

16 The mountains of Bashan are mighty mountains;
high-ridged mountains are the mountains of Bashan.
17 Why look with envy, you high-ridged mountains,
at the mountain where God has chosen to dwell?
It is there that the Lord shall dwell for ever.

18 The chariots of God are thousands upon thousands.
The Lord has come from Sinai to the holy place.
19 You have gone up on high; you have taken captives,
receiving men and women in tribute, O God,
even those who rebel, into your dwelling, O Lord.

20 May the Lord be blessed day after day.
He bears our burdens, God our savior;
21 this God of ours is a God who saves.
The Lord our God holds the keys of death.
22 And God will smite the head of his foes,
the crown of those who persist in their sins.

23 The Lord said: "I will bring them back from Bashan;
I will bring them back from the depth of the sea.
24 Then your feet will tread in their blood
and the tongues of your dogs take their share of the foe."

25 They see your solemn procession, O God,
the procession of my God, of my king, to the
sanctuary:
26 the singers in the forefront, the musicians
coming last,
between them, maidens sounding their timbrels.

27 "In festive gatherings, bless the Lord;
bless God, O you who are Israel's children."
28 There is Benjamin, least of the tribes, at the head,
Judah's leaders, a mighty throng,
Zebulun's leaders, Naphtali's leaders.

29 Show forth, O God, show forth your might,
your might, O God, which you have shown for us.
30 For the sake of your temple high in Jerusalem
may nations come to you bringing their tribute.

31 Threaten the wild beast that dwells in the reeds,
the bands of the mighty and rulers of the peoples.
Let them bow down offering silver.
Scatter the peoples who delight in war.
32 Envoys will make their way from Egypt;
Ethiopia will stretch out her hands to God.

33 Kingdoms of the earth, sing to God, praise the
Lord
34 who rides on the heavens, the ancient heavens.
He thunders his voice, his mighty voice.
35 Come, acknowledge the power of God.

His glory is on Israel; his might is in the skies.
36 God is to be feared in his holy place.
He is the Lord, Israel's God.
He gives strength and power to his people.

Blessed be God!

(68) 69. Cry from the depths of sorrow

2 Save me, O God,
for the waters have risen to my neck.

3 I have sunk into the mud of the deep
and there is no foothold.
I have entered the waters of the deep
and the waves overwhelm me.

4 I am wearied with all my crying,
my throat is parched.
My eyes are wasted away
from looking for my God.

5 More numerous than the hairs on my head
are those who hate me without cause.
Those who attack me with lies
are too much for my strength.

How can I restore
what I have never stolen?
6 O God, you know my sinful folly;
my sins you can see.

7 Let not those who hope in you be put to shame
through me, Lord of hosts;
let not those who seek you be dismayed
through me, God of Israel.

8 It is for you that I suffer taunts,
that shame covers my face,
9 that I have become a stranger to my family,
an alien to my brothers and sisters.
10 I burn with zeal for your house
and taunts against you fall on me.

11 When I afflict my soul with fasting
they make it a taunt against me.
12 When I put on sackcloth in mourning
then they make me a byword,
13 the gossip of folk at the gates,
the subject of drunkards' songs.

14 This is my prayer to you,
my prayer for your favor.
In your great love, answer me, O God,
with your help that never fails;
15 rescue me from sinking in the mud,
save me from my foes.

Save me from the waters of the deep
16 lest the waves overwhelm me.
Do not let the deep engulf me
nor death close its mouth on me.

17 Lord, answer, for your love is kind;
in your compassion, turn towards me.
18 Do not hide your face from your servant;
answer quickly for I am in distress.
19 Come close to my soul and redeem me;
ransom me pressed by my foes.

20 You know how they taunt and deride me;
my oppressors are all before you.
21 Taunts have broken my heart;
I have reached the end of my strength.
I looked in vain for compassion,
for consolers; not one could I find.

22 For food they gave me poison;
in my thirst they gave me vinegar to drink.
23 Let their table be a snare to them
and their festive banquets a trap.
24 Let their eyes grow dim and blind;
let their limbs tremble and shake.

25 Pour out your anger upon them,
let the heat of your fury overtake them.
26 Let their camp be left desolate;
let no one dwell in their tents;
27 for they persecute one whom you struck;
they increase the pain of one you wounded.

28 Charge them with guilt upon guilt;
let them never be found just in your sight.
29 Blot them out from the book of the living;
do not enroll them among the just.
30 As for me in my poverty and pain,
let your help, O God, lift me up.

31 I will praise God's name with a song;
I will glorify him with thanksgiving.
32 A gift pleasing God more than oxen,
more than beasts prepared for sacrifice.

33 The poor when they see it will be glad
and God-seeking hearts will revive;
34 for the Lord listens to the needy
and does not spurn his servants in their chains.
35 Let the heavens and the earth give him praise,
the sea and all its living creatures.

36 For God will bring help to Zion
and rebuild the cities of Judah
and people shall dwell there in possession.
37 The children of his servants shall inherit it;
those who love his name shall dwell there.

(69) 70. A prayer for help against enemies

2 O God, make haste to my rescue,
Lord, come to my aid!
3 Let there be shame and confusion
on those who seek my life.

O let them turn back in confusion,
who delight in my harm;
4 let them retreat, covered with shame,
who jeer at my lot.

5 Let there be rejoicing and gladness
for all who seek you.
Let them say for ever: "God is great,"
who love your saving help.

6 As for me, wretched and poor,
come to me, O God.
You are my rescuer, my help,
O Lord, do not delay.

(70) 71. A prayer in old age

1 In you, O Lord, I take refuge;
let me never be put to shame.
2 In your justice rescue me, free me;
pay heed to me and save me.

3 Be a rock where I can take refuge,
a mighty stronghold to save me;
for you are my rock, my stronghold.
4 Free me from the hand of the wicked,
from the grip of the unjust, of the oppressor.

5 It is you, O Lord, who are my hope,
my trust, O Lord, since my youth.
6 On you I have leaned from my birth;
from my mother's womb you have been my help.
My hope has always been in you.

7 My fate has filled many with awe
but you are my strong refuge.
8 My lips are filled with your praise,
with your glory all the day long.
9 Do not reject me now that I am old;
when my strength fails do not forsake me.

10 For my enemies are speaking about me;
those who watch me take counsel together.
11 They say that God has forsaken me,
they can seize me and no one will save me.
12 O God, do not stay far off:
my God, make haste to help me!

13 Let them be put to shame and destroyed,
all those who seek my life.
Let them be covered with shame and confusion,
all those who seek to harm me.

14 But as for me, I will always hope
and praise you more and more.
15 My lips will tell of your justice
and day by day of your help
(though I can never tell it all).

16 Lord, I will declare your mighty deeds,
proclaiming your justice, yours alone.
17 O God, you have taught me from my youth
and I proclaim your wonders still.

18 Now that I am old and grey-headed,
do not forsake me, God.
Let me tell of your power to all ages,
praise your strength 19 and justice to the skies,
tell of you who have worked such wonders.
O God, who is like you?

20 You have burdened me with bitter troubles
but you will give me back my life.
You will raise me from the depths of the earth;
21 you will exalt me and console me again.

22 So I will give you thanks on the lyre
for your faithful love, my God.
To you will I sing with the harp,
to you, the Holy One of Israel.
23 When I sing to you my lips shall rejoice
and my soul, which you have redeemed.

24 And all the day long my tongue
shall tell the tale of your justice:
for they are put to shame and disgraced,
all those who seek to harm me.

(71) 72. The kingdom of peace

1 O God, give your judgment to the king,
to a king's son your justice,
2 that he may judge your people in justice
and your poor in right judgment.

3 May the mountains bring forth peace for the people
and the hills, justice.
4 May he defend the poor of the people
and save the children of the needy
(and crush the oppressor).

5 He shall endure like the sun and the moon
from age to age.
6 He shall descend like rain on the meadow,
like raindrops on the earth.

7 In his days justice shall flourish
and peace till the moon fails.
8 He shall rule from sea to sea,
from the Great River to earth's bounds.

9 Before him his enemies shall fall,
his foes lick the dust.
10 The kings of Tarshish and the seacoasts
shall pay him tribute.

The kings of Sheba and Seba
shall bring him gifts.
11 Before him all rulers shall fall prostrate,
all nations shall serve him.

12 For he shall save the poor when they cry
and the needy who are helpless.
13 He will have pity on the weak
and save the lives of the poor.

14 From oppression he will rescue their lives,
to him their blood is dear.
15 (Long may he live,
may the gold of Sheba be given him.)

They shall pray for him without ceasing
and bless him all the day.

16 May corn be abundant in the land
to the peaks of the mountains.
May its fruit rustle like Lebanon;
may people flourish in the cities
like grass on the earth.

17 May his name be blessed for ever
and endure like the sun.
Every tribe shall be blessed in him,
all nations bless his name.

* * * * *

18 Blessed be the Lord, God of Israel,
who alone works wonders,
19 ever blessed his glorious name.
Let his glory fill the earth.

Amen! Amen!

(72) 73. The problem of innocent suffering

1 How good is God to Israel,
to those who are pure of heart.
2 Yet my feet came close to stumbling,
my steps had almost slipped
3 for I was filled with envy of the proud
when I saw how the wicked prosper.

4 For them there are no pains;
their bodies are sound and sleek.
5 They do not share in human sorrows;
they are not stricken like others.

6 So they wear their pride like a necklace,
they clothe themselves with violence.
7 Their hearts overflow with malice,
their minds seethe with plots.

8 They scoff; they speak with malice;
from on high they plan oppression.
9 They have set their mouths in the heavens
and their tongues dictate to the earth.

10 So the people turn to follow them
and drink in all their words.
11 They say: "How can God know?
Does the Most High take any notice?"
12 Look at them, such are the wicked,
but untroubled, they grow in wealth.

* * * * *

13 How useless to keep my heart pure
and wash my hands in innocence,
14 when I was stricken all day long,
suffered punishment day after day.

15 Then I said: "If I should speak like that,
I should betray all my ancestors."

16 I strove to fathom this problem,
too hard for my mind to understand,
17 until I pierced the mysteries of God
and understood what becomes of the wicked.

* * * * *

18 How slippery the paths on which you set them;
you make them slide to destruction.
19 How suddenly they come to their ruin,
wiped out, destroyed by terrors.
20 Like a dream one wakes from, O Lord,
when you wake you dismiss them as phantoms.

21 And so when my heart grew embittered
and when I was cut to the quick,
22 I was stupid and did not understand,
no better than a beast in your sight.

23 Yet I was always in your presence;
you were holding me by my right hand.
24 You will guide me by your counsel
and so you will lead me to glory.

25 What else have I in heaven but you?
Apart from you I want nothing on earth.
26 My body and my heart faint for joy;
God is my possession for ever.

27 All those who abandon you shall perish;
you will destroy all those who are faithless.
28 To be near God is my happiness.
I have made the Lord God my refuge.
I will tell of all your works
at the gates of the city of Zion.

(73) 74. God's people mourn over the ruined temple: a national lament

1 Why, O God, have you cast us off for ever?
Why blaze with anger at the sheep of your
pasture?

2 Remember your people whom you chose
long ago,
the tribe you redeemed to be your own
possession,
the mountains of Zion where you made
your dwelling.

3 Turn your steps to these places that are utterly
ruined!
The enemy has laid waste the whole of the
sanctuary.
4 Your foes have made uproar in your house
of prayer;
they have set up their emblems, their foreign
emblems,
5 high above the entrance to the sanctuary.

Their axes 6 have battered the wood of its doors.
They have struck together with hatchet and
pickaxe.
7 O God, they have set your sanctuary on fire;
they have razed and profaned the place where
you dwell.
8 They said in their hearts: "Let us utterly crush
them;
let us burn every shrine of God in the land."
9 There is no sign from God, nor have we a
prophet,
we have no one to tell us how long it will last.

10 How long, O God, is the enemy to scoff?
Is the foe to insult your name for ever?
11 Why, O Lord, do you hold back your hand?
Why do you keep your right hand hidden?

12 Yet God is our king from time past,
the giver of help through all the land.
13 It was you who divided the sea by your might,
who shattered the heads of the monsters in
the sea.

14 It was you who crushed Leviathan's heads
and gave him as food to the untamed beasts.
15 It was you who opened springs and torrents;
it was you who dried up ever-flowing rivers.

16 Yours is the day and yours is the night.
It was you who appointed the light and the sun;
17 it was you who fixed the bounds of the earth;
you who made both summer and winter.

18 Remember this, Lord, and see the enemy
scoffing;
a senseless people insults your name.
19 Do not give Israel, your dove, to the hawk
nor forget the life of your poor ones for ever.

20 Remember your covenant; every cave in the land
is a place where violence makes its home.
21 Do not let the oppressed return disappointed;
let the poor and the needy bless your name.

22 Arise, O God, and defend your cause!
Remember how the senseless revile you all
the day.
23 Do not forget the clamor of your foes,
the daily increasing uproar of your foes.

(74) 75. God, the judge of the world

2 We give thanks to you, O God,
we give thanks and call upon your name.
We recount your wonderful deeds.

* * * * *

3 "When I reach the appointed time,
then I will judge with justice.
4 Though the earth and all who dwell in it
may rock,
it is I who uphold its pillars.

5 To the boastful I say: 'Do not boast,'
to the wicked: 'Do not flaunt your strength,
6 do not flaunt your strength on high.
Do not speak with insolent pride.' "

7 For neither from the east nor the west,
nor from desert or mountains comes judgment,
8 but God himself is the judge.
One he humbles, another he exalts.

9 The Lord holds a cup in his hand,
full of wine, foaming and spiced.
He pours it; they drink it to the dregs;
all the wicked on the earth must drain it.

10 As for me, I will rejoice for ever
and sing psalms to Jacob's God.
11 He shall break the power of the wicked,
while the strength of the just shall be exalted.

(75) 76. Thanksgiving after victory

2 God, you are made known in Judah;
in Israel your name is great.
3 You set up your tent in Jerusalem
and your dwelling place in Zion.
4 It was there you broke the flashing arrows,
the shield, the sword, the armor.

5 You, O Lord, are resplendent,
more majestic than the everlasting mountains.
6 The warriors, despoiled, slept in death;
the hands of the soldiers were powerless.
7 At your threat, O God of Jacob,
horse and rider lay stunned.

8 You, you alone, strike terror.
Who shall stand when your anger is roused?
9 You uttered your sentence from the heavens;
the earth in terror was still
10 when you arose to judge,
to save the humble of the earth.

11 Human anger will serve to praise you;
those who survive it rejoice in you.
12 Make vows to your God and fulfill them.
Let all pay tribute to him who strikes terror,
13 who cuts short the breath of rulers,
who strikes terror in the leaders of the earth.

(76) 77. God and his people: the lessons of past history

2 I cry aloud to God,
cry aloud to God that he may hear me.

3 In the day of my distress I sought the Lord.
My hands were raised at night without ceasing;
my soul refused to be consoled.
4 I remembered my God and I groaned.
I pondered and my spirit fainted.

5 You withheld sleep from my eyes.
I was troubled, I could not speak.
6 I thought of the days of long ago
and remembered the years long past.
7 At night I mused within my heart.
I pondered and my spirit questioned.

8 "Will the Lord reject us for ever?
Will he show us his favor no more?
9 Has his love vanished for ever?
Has his promise come to an end?
10 Does God forget his mercy
or in anger withhold his compassion?"

11 I said: "This is what causes my grief,
that the way of the Most High has changed."
12 I remember the deeds of the Lord,
I remember your wonders of old,
13 I muse on all your works
and ponder your mighty deeds.

14 Your ways, O God, are holy.
What god is great as our God?
15 You are the God who works wonders.
You showed your power among the peoples.
16 Your strong arm redeemed your people,
the children of Jacob and Joseph.

17 The waters saw you, O God,
the waters saw you and trembled;
the depths were moved with terror.
18 The clouds poured down rain,
the skies sent forth their voice;
your arrows flashed to and fro.

19 Your thunder rolled round the sky,
your flashes lighted up the world.
The earth was moved and trembled
20 when your way led through the sea,
your path through the mighty waters
and no one saw your footprints.

21 You guided your people like a flock
by the hand of Moses and Aaron.

(77) 78. God's patience and man's ingratitude: the past and the present

1 Give heed, my people, to my teaching;
turn your ear to the words of my mouth.
2 I will open my mouth in a parable
and reveal hidden lessons of the past.

3 The things we have heard and understood,
the things our forebears have told us,
4 these we will not hide from their children
but will tell them to the next generation:

the glories of the Lord and his might
and the marvelous deeds he has done,
5 the witness he gave to Jacob,
the law he established in Israel.

He gave a command to our forebears
to make it known to their children
6 that the next generation might know it,
the ones yet to be born.
7 They too should arise and tell their children
that they too should set their hope in God
and never forget God's deeds
but keep every one of his commands,

8 so that they might not be like their forebears,
a people rebellious and stubborn,
a people whose heart was fickle,
whose spirit was unfaithful to God.

* * * * *

9 Ephraim's people, armed with the bow,
turned back in the day of battle.
10 They failed to keep God's covenant
and would not walk according to his law.

11 They forgot the things he had done,
the marvelous deeds he had shown them.
12 He did wonders in the sight of their forebears,
in Egypt, in the plains of Zoan.

13 He divided the sea and led them through
and made the waters stand up like a wall.
14 By day he led them with a cloud,
by night, with a light of fire.

15 He split the rocks in the desert.
He gave them plentiful drink as from the deep.
16 He made streams flow out from the rock
and made waters run down like rivers.

* * * * *

17 Yet still they sinned against him;
they defied the Most High in the desert.
18 In their heart they put God to the test
by demanding the food they craved.

19 They even spoke against God.
They said: "Is it possible for God
to prepare a table in the desert?

20 It was he who struck the rock,
water flowed and swept down in torrents.
But can he also give us bread?
Can he provide meat for his people?"

21 When he heard this the Lord was angry.
A fire was kindled against Jacob,
his anger rose against Israel
22 for having no faith in God;
for refusing to trust in his help.

23 Yet he commanded the clouds above
and opened the gates of heaven.
24 He rained down manna for their food,
and gave them bread from heaven.

25 Mere mortals ate the food of angels.
He sent them meat in abundance;
26 he made the east wind blow from heaven
and roused the south wind by his might.

27 He rained food on them like dust,
winged fowl like the sands of the sea.
28 He let it fall in the midst of their camp
and all around their tents.

29 So they ate and had their fill;
and he gave them all they craved.
30 But before they had sated their craving,
while the food was still in their mouths,

31 God's anger rose against them.
He slew the strongest among them,
struck down the flower of Israel.

32 Despite this they went on sinning;
they had no faith in his wonders:
33 so he ended their days like a breath
and their years in sudden ruin.

34 When he slew them then they would seek him,
return and seek him in earnest.
35 They would remember that God was their rock,
God the Most High their redeemer.

36 But the words they spoke were mere flattery;
they lied to him with their lips.
37 For their hearts were not truly with him;
they were not faithful to his covenant.

38 Yet he who is full of compassion
forgave them their sin and spared them.
So often he held back his anger
when he might have stirred up his rage.

39 He remembered they were only human,
a breath that passes never to return.

* * * * *

40 How often they defied him in the wilderness
and caused him pain in the desert!

41 Yet again they put God to the test
and grieved the Holy One of Israel.
42 They did not remember his deeds
nor the day he saved them from the foe;

43 when he worked his miracles in Egypt,
his wonders in the plains of Zoan;
44 when he turned their rivers into blood,
made their streams impossible to drink.

45 He sent dogflies against them to devour them
and swarms of frogs to molest them.
46 He gave their crops to the grub,
the fruit of their labor to the locust.

47 He destroyed their vines with hail,
their sycamore trees with frost.
48 He gave up their cattle to plague,
their flocks and herds to pestilence.

49 He turned on them the heat of his anger,
fury, rage and havoc,
a troop of destroying angels.
50 He gave free course to his anger.

He did not spare them from death
but gave their lives to the plague.
51 He struck all the first-born in Egypt,
the finest flower in the dwellings of Ham.

52 Then he brought forth his people like sheep;
he guided his flock in the desert.
53 He led them safely with nothing to fear,
while the sea engulfed their foes.

54 So he brought them to his holy land,
to the mountain which his right hand had won.
55 He drove out the nations before them,
and divided the land for their heritage.

Their tents he gave as a dwelling
to each one of Israel's tribes.

* * * * *

56 Still they put God to the proof and defied him;
they refused to obey the Most High.

57 They strayed, faithless like their forebears,
like a bow on which the archer cannot count.
58 With their mountain shrines they angered him;
made him jealous with the idols they served.

59 God saw and was filled with fury;
he utterly rejected Israel.
60 He forsook his dwelling place in Shiloh,
the tent where he lived among his people.

61 He gave his ark into captivity,
his glorious ark into the hands of the foe.
62 He gave up his people to the sword,
in his anger against his chosen ones.

63 So war devoured their young men,
their maidens had no wedding songs;
64 their priests fell by the sword,
their widows made no lamentation.

65 Then the Lord awoke as if from sleep,
like a warrior overcome with wine.
66 He struck his foes from behind
and put them to everlasting shame.

67 He rejected the tent of Joseph;
he did not choose the tribe of Ephraim
68 but he chose the tribe of Judah,
the hill of Zion which he loves.

69 He built his shrine like the heavens,
or like the earth which he made firm for ever.
70 And he chose David his servant
and took him away from the sheepfolds.

71 From the care of the ewes he called him
to be shepherd of Jacob his people,
of Israel his own possession.
72 He tended them with blameless heart,
with discerning mind he led them.

(78) 79. National lament over the destruction of Jerusalem

1 O God, the nations have invaded your land,
they have profaned your holy temple.
They have made Jerusalem a heap of ruins.
2 They have handed over the bodies of your
servants
as food to feed the birds of heaven
and the flesh of your faithful to the beasts
of the earth.

3 They have poured out blood like water in
Jerusalem;
no one is left to bury the dead.
4 We have become the taunt of our neighbors,
the mockery and scorn of those who surround us.
5 How long, O Lord? Will you be angry for ever;
how long will your anger burn like fire?

6 Pour out your rage on the nations,
the nations that do not know you.
Pour out your rage on the kingdoms
that do not call on your name,
7 for they have destroyed the family of Jacob
and laid waste the land where they dwell.

8 Do not blame us for the sins of our forebears.
Let your compassion hasten to meet us;
we are left in the depths of distress.
9 O God our savior, come to our help,
come for the sake of the glory of your name.
O Lord our God, forgive us our sins;
rescue us for the sake of your name.

10 Why should the nations say: "Where is their
God?"
Let us see the nations around us repaid
with vengeance for the blood of your servants
that was shed!
11 Let the groans of the prisoners come before you;
let your strong arm reprieve those condemned
to die.

12 Pay back to our neighbors seven times over
the taunts with which they taunted you, O Lord.
13 But we, your people, the flock of your pasture,
will give you thanks for ever and ever.
We will tell your praise from age to age.

(79) 80. The ravaged vine

2 O shepherd of Israel, hear us,
you who lead Joseph's flock,
shine forth from your cherubim throne
3 upon Ephraim, Benjamin, Manasseh.

O Lord, rouse up your might,
O Lord, come to our help.

4 God of hosts, bring us back;
let your face shine on us and we shall be saved.

5 Lord God of hosts, how long
will you frown on your people's plea?
6 You have fed them with tears for their bread,
and abundance of tears for their drink.
7 You have made us the taunt of our neighbors,
our enemies laugh us to scorn.

8 God of hosts, bring us back;
let your face shine on us and we shall be saved.

9 You brought a vine out of Egypt;
to plant it you drove out the nations.
10 Before it you cleared the ground;
it took root and spread through the land.

11 The mountains were covered with its shadow,
the cedars of God with its boughs.
12 It stretched out its branches to the sea,
to the Great River it stretched out its shoots.

13 Then why have you broken down its walls?
It is plucked by all who pass by.
14 It is ravaged by the boar of the forest,
devoured by the beasts of the field.

15 God of hosts, turn again, we implore,
look down from heaven and see.
Visit the vine 16 and protect it.
the vine your right hand has planted.
17 They have burnt it with fire and destroyed it.
May they perish at the frown of your face.

18 May your hand be on the one you have chosen,
the one you have given your strength.
19 And we shall never forsake you again;
give us life that we may call upon your name.

20 God of hosts, bring us back;
let your face shine on us and we shall be saved.

(80) 81. A festal song for harvest time

2 Ring out your joy to God our strength,
shout in triumph to the God of Jacob.

3 Raise a song and sound the timbrel,
the sweet-sounding harp and the lute;
4 blow the trumpet at the new moon,
when the moon is full, on our feast.

5 For this is Israel's law,
a command of the God of Jacob.
6 He imposed it as a law on Joseph's people,
when he went out against the land of Egypt.

A voice I did not know said to me:
7 "I freed your shoulder from the burden;
your hands were freed from the load.
8 You called in distress and I saved you.

I answered, concealed in the storm cloud;
at the waters of Meribah I tested you.
9 Listen, my people, to my warning.
O Israel, if only you would heed!

10 Let there be no foreign god among you,
no worship of an alien god.
11 I am the Lord your God,
who brought you from the land of Egypt.
Open wide your mouth and I will fill it.

12 But my people did not heed my voice
and Israel would not obey,
13 so I left them in their stubbornness of heart
to follow their own designs.

14 O that my people would heed me,
that Israel would walk in my ways!
15 At once I would subdue their foes,
turn my hand against their enemies.

16 The Lord's enemies would cringe at their feet
and their subjection would last for ever.
But Israel I would feed with finest wheat
and fill them with honey from the rock."

(81) 82. God's judgment on corrupt authority

1 God stands in the divine assembly.
In the midst of the gods he gives judgment.

2 "How long will you judge unjustly
and favor the cause of the wicked?
3 Do justice for the weak and the orphan,
defend the afflicted and the needy.
4 Rescue the weak and the poor;
set them free from the hand of the wicked.

5 Unperceiving, they grope in the darkness
and the order of the world is shaken.
6 I have said: 'You call yourselves gods
and all of you, children of the Most High.'
7 And yet, you shall die like mortals,
you shall fall like any earthly ruler."

8 Arise, O God, judge the earth,
for you rule all the nations.

(82) 83. A nation's appeal to God for help against destruction

2 O God, do not keep silent,
do not be dumb and unmoved, O God,
3 for your enemies raise a tumult.
Those who hate you lift up their heads.

4 They plot against your people,
conspire against those you love.
5 They say: "Come, let us destroy them as a nation;
let the name of Israel be forgotten."
6 They conspire with a single mind,
they make common alliance against you,

7 the camps of Edom and of Ishmael,
the camps of Moab and Hagar,
8 the land of Ammon and Amalek,
Philistia, with the people of Tyre.
9 Assyria, too, is their ally
and joins hands with the children of Lot.

10 Treat them like Midian, like Sisera,
like Jabin at the River Kishon,
11 the men who were destroyed at Endor,
whose bodies rotted on the ground.

12 Make their captains like Oreb and Zeëb,
all their princes like Zebah and Zalmunna,
13 the men who said: "Let us take
the fields of God for ourselves."
14 My God, scatter them like chaff,
drive them like straw in the wind!

15 As fire that burns away the forest,
as the flame that sets the mountains ablaze,
16 drive them away with your tempest
and fill them with terror at your storm.
17 Cover their faces with shame,
till they seek your name, O Lord.

18 Shame and terror be theirs for ever;
let them be disgraced, let them perish!
19 Let them know that your name is the Lord,
the Most High over all the earth.

(83) 84. Longing for God's temple

2 How lovely is your dwelling place,
Lord, God of hosts.

3 My soul is longing and yearning,
is yearning for the courts of the Lord.
My heart and my soul ring out their joy
to God, the living God.

4 The sparrow herself finds a home
and the swallow a nest for her brood;
she lays her young by your altars,
Lord of hosts, my king and my God.

5 They are happy, who dwell in your house,
for ever singing your praise.
6 They are happy, whose strength is in you,
in whose hearts are the roads to Zion.

7 As they go through the Bitter Valley
they make it a place of springs,
(the autumn rain covers it with blessings).
8 They walk with ever growing strength,
they will see the God of gods in Zion.

9 O Lord God of hosts, hear my prayer,
give ear, O God of Jacob.
10 Turn your eyes, O God, our shield,
look on the face of your anointed.

11 One day within your courts
is better than a thousand elsewhere.
The threshold of the house of God
I prefer to the dwellings of the wicked.

12 For the Lord God is a rampart, a shield;
he will give us his favor and glory.
The Lord will not refuse any good
to those who walk without blame.

13 Lord, God of hosts,
happy are those who trust in you!

(84) 85. The coming age of peace and justice

2 O Lord, you once favored your land
and revived the fortunes of Jacob,
3 you forgave the guilt of your people
and covered all their sins.

4 You averted all your rage,
you calmed the heat of your anger.

5 Revive us now, God, our helper!
Put an end to your grievance against us.
6 Will you be angry with us for ever,
will your anger never cease?

7 Will you not restore again our life
that your people may rejoice in you?
8 Let us see, O Lord, your mercy
and give us your saving help.

* * * * *

9 I will hear what the Lord God has to say,
a voice that speaks of peace,
peace for his people and his friends
and those who turn to him in their hearts.
10 His help is near for those who fear him
and his glory will dwell in our land.

11 Mercy and faithfulness have met;
justice and peace have embraced.
12 Faithfulness shall spring from the earth
and justice look down from heaven.

13 The Lord will make us prosper
and our earth shall yield its fruit.
14 Justice shall march before him
and peace shall follow his steps.

(85) 86. Loyalty in God's service

1 Turn your ear, O Lord, and give answer
for I am poor and needy.

2 Preserve my life, for I am faithful;
save the servant who trusts in you.

3 You are my God, have mercy on me, Lord,
for I cry to you all the day long.
4 Give joy to your servant, O Lord,
for to you I lift up my soul.

5 O Lord, you are good and forgiving,
full of love to all who call.
6 Give heed, O Lord, to my prayer
and attend to the sound of my voice.

7 In the day of distress I will call
and surely you will reply.
8 Among the gods there is none like you, O Lord,
nor work to compare with yours.

9 All the nations shall come to adore you
and glorify your name, O Lord,
10 for you are great and do marvelous deeds,
you who alone are God.

11 Show me, Lord, your way
so that I may walk in your truth.
Guide my heart to fear your name.

12 I will praise you, Lord my God, with all my heart
and glorify your name for ever;
13 for your love to me has been great,
you have saved me from the depths of the grave.

14 The proud have risen against me;
ruthless enemies seek my life;
to you they pay no heed.

15 But you, God of mercy and compassion,
slow to anger, O Lord,
abounding in love and truth,
16 turn and take pity on me.

O give your strength to your servant
and save your handmaid's child.
17 Show me a sign of your favor
that my foes may see to their shame
that you console me and give me your help.

(86) 87. God's city, mother of all nations

1 On the holy mountain is his city
2 cherished by the Lord.
The Lord prefers the gates of Zion
to all Jacob's dwellings.
3 Of you are told glorious things,
O city of God!

4 "Babylon and Egypt I will count
among those who know me;
Philistia, Tyre, Ethiopia,
these will be her children
5 and Zion shall be called 'Mother'
for all shall be her children."

It is he, the Lord Most High,
who gives each a place.
6 In his register of peoples God writes:
"These are her children,"
7 and while they dance they will sing:
"In you all find their home."

(87) 88. A prayer in desolation

2 Lord my God, I call for help by day;
I cry at night before you.
3 Let my prayer come into your presence.
O turn your ear to my cry.

4 For my soul is filled with evils;
my life is on the brink of the grave.
5 I am reckoned as one in the tomb;
I have reached the end of my strength,

6 like one alone among the dead,
like the slain lying in their graves,
like those you remember no more,
cut off, as they are, from your hand.

7 You have laid me in the depths of the tomb,
in places that are dark, in the depths.
8 Your anger weighs down upon me;
I am drowned beneath your waves.

9 You have taken away my friends
and made me hateful in their sight.
Imprisoned, I cannot escape;
10 my eyes are sunken with grief.

I call to you, Lord, all the day long;
to you I stretch out my hands.
11 Will you work your wonders for the dead?
Will the shades stand and praise you?

12 Will your love be told in the grave
or your faithfulness among the dead?
13 Will your wonders be known in the dark
or your justice in the land of oblivion?

14 As for me, Lord, I call to you for help;
in the morning my prayer comes before you.
15 Lord, why do you reject me?
Why do you hide your face?

16 Wretched, close to death from my youth,
I have borne your trials; I am numb.
17 Your fury has swept down upon me;
your terrors have utterly destroyed me.

18 They surround me all the day like a flood,
they assail me all together.
19 Friend and neighbor you have taken away;
my one companion is darkness.

(88) 89. Will God break his promises?

2 I will sing for ever of your love, O Lord;
through all ages my mouth will proclaim
your truth.
3 Of this I am sure, that your love lasts for ever,
that your truth is firmly established as the
heavens.

4 "With my chosen one I have made a covenant;
I have sworn to David my servant:
5 I will establish your dynasty for ever
and set up your throne through all ages."

6 The heavens proclaim your wonders, O Lord;
the assembly of your holy ones proclaims
your truth.
7 For who in the skies can compare with the Lord
or who is like the Lord among the children
of God?

8 A God to be feared in the council of the holy
ones,
great and dreadful to all around him.
9 O Lord God of hosts, who is your equal?
You are mighty, O Lord, and truth is your
garment.

10 It is you who rule the sea in its pride;
it is you who still the surging of its waves.
11 It is you who trod Rahab underfoot like a corpse,
scattering your foes with your mighty arm.

12 The heavens are yours, the world is yours.
It is you who founded the earth and all it holds;
13 it is you who created the North and the South.
Tabor and Hermon shout for joy at your name.

14 Yours is a mighty arm, O Lord;
your hand is strong, your right hand ready.
15 Justice and right are the pillars of your throne,
love and truth walk in your presence.

16 Happy the people who acclaim such a God,
who walk, O Lord, in the light of your face,
17 who find their joy every day in your name,
who make your justice the source of their bliss.

18 For you, O Lord, are the glory of their strength;
by your favor it is that our might is exalted;
19 for our ruler is in the keeping of the Lord;
our king in the keeping of the Holy One of Israel.

* * * * *

20 Of old you spoke in a vision.
To your friends the prophets you said:

"I have set the crown on a warrior,
I have exalted one chosen from the people.

21 I have found David my servant
and with my holy oil anointed him.
22 My hand shall always be with him
and my arm shall make him strong.

23 The enemy shall never outwit him
nor the evil ones oppress him.
24 I will beat down his foes before him
and smite those who hate him.

25 My truth and my love shall be with him;
by my name his might shall be exalted.
26 I will stretch out his hand to the Sea
and his right hand as far as the River.

27 He will say to me: 'You are my father,
my God, the rock who saves me!'
28 And I will make him my first-born,
the highest of the kings of the earth.

29 I will keep my love for him always;
with him my covenant shall last.
30 I will establish his dynasty for ever,
make his throne endure as the heavens.

31 If his children forsake my law
and refuse to walk as I decree
32 and if ever they violate my statutes,
refusing to keep my commands;

33 then I will punish their offenses with the rod,
then I will scourge them on account of their guilt.
34 But I will never take back my love,
my truth will never fail.

35 I will never violate my covenant
nor go back on the word I have spoken.
36 Once for all, I have sworn by my holiness.
'I will never lie to David.
37 His dynasty shall last for ever.
In my sight his throne is like the sun;
38 like the moon, it shall endure for ever,
a faithful witness in the skies.' "

* * * * *

39 And yet you have spurned, rejected,
you are angry with the one you have anointed.
40 You have broken your covenant with your servant
and dishonored his crown in the dust.

41 You have broken down all his walls
and reduced his fortresses to ruins.
42 He is despoiled by all who pass by;
he has become the taunt of his neighbors.

43 You have exalted the right hand of his foes;
you have made all his enemies rejoice.
44 You have made his sword give way,
you have not upheld him in battle.

45 You have brought his glory to an end;
you have hurled his throne to the ground.
46 You have cut short the years of his youth;
you have heaped disgrace upon him.

47 How long, O Lord? Will you hide yourself for
ever?
How long will your anger burn like a fire?
48 Remember, Lord, the shortness of my life
and how frail you have made all human beings.

49 Who can live and never see death?
Who can save themselves from the grasp of
the grave?

50 Where are your mercies of the past, O Lord,
which you have sworn in your faithfulness
to David?
51 Remember, Lord, how your servant is taunted,
how I have to bear all the insults of the peoples.
52 Thus your enemies taunt me, O Lord,
mocking your anointed at every step.

* * * * *

53 Blessed be the Lord for ever. Amen, amen!

(89) 90. God's eternity and the shortness of life

1 O Lord, you have been our refuge
from one generation to the next.
2 Before the mountains were born
or the earth or the world brought forth,
you are God, without beginning or end.

3 You turn us back into dust
and say: "Go back, children of the earth."
4 To your eyes a thousand years
are like yesterday, come and gone,
no more than a watch in the night.

5 You sweep us away like a dream,
like grass which springs up in the morning.
6 In the morning it springs up and flowers;
by evening it withers and fades.

7 So we are destroyed in your anger,
struck with terror in your fury.
8 Our guilt lies open before you,
our secrets in the light of your face.

9 All our days pass away in your anger.
Our life is over like a sigh.
10 Our span is seventy years,
or eighty for those who are strong.

And most of these are emptiness and pain.
They pass swiftly and we are gone.
11 Who understands the power of your anger
and fears the strength of your fury?

12 Make us know the shortness of our life
that we may gain wisdom of heart.
13 Lord, relent! Is your anger for ever?
Show pity to your servants.

14 In the morning, fill us with your love;
we shall exult and rejoice all our days.
15 Give us joy to balance our affliction
for the years when we knew misfortune.

16 Show forth your work to your servants;
let your glory shine on their children.
17 Let the favor of the Lord be upon us:
give success to the work of our hands
(give success to the work of our hands).

(90) 91. Under the wing of God's protection

1 Those who dwell in the shelter of the Most High
and abide in the shade of the Almighty

2 say to the Lord: "My refuge,
my stronghold, my God in whom I trust!"

3 It is he who will free you from the snare
of the fowler who seeks to destroy you;
4 he will conceal you with his pinions
and under his wings you will find refuge.

5 You will not fear the terror of the night
nor the arrow that flies by day,
6 nor the plague that prowls in the darkness
nor the scourge that lays waste at noon.

7 A thousand may fall at your side,
ten thousand fall at your right,
you, it will never approach;
4c his faithfulness is buckler and shield.

8 Your eyes have only to look
to see how the wicked are repaid,
9 you who have said: "Lord, my refuge!"
and have made the Most High your dwelling.

10 Upon you no evil shall fall,
no plague approach where you dwell.
11 For you has he commanded his angels,
to keep you in all your ways.

12 They shall bear you upon their hands
lest you strike your foot against a stone.
13 On the lion and the viper you will tread
and trample the young lion and the dragon.

14 You set your love on me so I will save you,
protect you for you know my name.
15 When you call I shall answer: "I am with you,"
I will save you in distress and give you glory.

16 With length of days I will content you;
I shall let you see my saving power.

(91) 92. Praise of God's justice

2 It is good to give thanks to the Lord,
to make music to your name, O Most High,
3 to proclaim your love in the morning
and your truth in the watches of the night,
4 on the ten-stringed lyre and the lute,
with the murmuring sound of the harp.

5 Your deeds, O Lord, have made me glad;
for the work of your hands I shout with joy.
6 O Lord, how great are your works!
How deep are your designs!
7 The stupid cannot know this
and the foolish cannot understand.

8 Though the wicked spring up like grass
and all who do evil thrive,
they are doomed to be eternally destroyed.
9 But you, Lord, are eternally on high.
10 See how your enemies perish;
all doers of evil are scattered.

11 To me you give the wild ox's strength;
you anoint me with the purest oil.
12 My eyes looked in triumph on my foes;
my ears heard gladly of their fall.
13 The just will flourish like the palm tree
and grow like a Lebanon cedar.

14 Planted in the house of the Lord
they will flourish in the courts of our God,
15 still bearing fruit when they are old,
still full of sap, still green,
16 to proclaim that the Lord is just.
In him, my rock, there is no wrong.

(92) 93. God, king of the world

1 The Lord is king, with majesty enrobed;
the Lord has robed himself with might,
he has girded himself with power.

The world you made firm, not to be moved;
2 your throne has stood firm from of old.
From all eternity, O Lord, you are.

3 The waters have lifted up, O Lord,
the waters have lifted up their voice,
the waters have lifted up their thunder.

4 Greater than the roar of mighty waters,
more glorious than the surgings of the sea,
the Lord is glorious on high.

5 Truly your decrees are to be trusted.
Holiness is fitting to your house,
O Lord, until the end of time.

(93) 94. God the judge of all

1 O Lord, avenging God,
avenging God, appear!
2 Judge of the earth, arise,
give the proud what they deserve!

3 How long, O Lord, shall the wicked,
how long shall the wicked triumph?
4 They bluster with arrogant speech;
the evildoers boast to each other.

5 They crush your people, Lord,
they afflict the ones you have chosen.
6 They kill the widow and the stranger
and murder the orphaned child.

7 And they say: "The Lord does not see;
the God of Jacob pays no heed."
8 Mark this, most senseless of people;
fools, when will you understand?

9 Can he who made the ear, not hear?
Can he who formed the eye, not see?

10 Will he who trains nations not punish?
Will he who instructs us not have knowledge?
11 (The Lord knows the thoughts of men and
women.
He knows they are no more than a breath.)

12 Happy those whom you teach, O Lord,
whom you train by means of your law;
to them you give peace in evil days
while the pit is being dug for the wicked.

14 The Lord will not abandon his people
nor forsake those who are his own;
15 for judgment shall again be just
and all true hearts shall uphold it.

16 Who will stand up for me against the wicked?
Who will defend me from those who do evil?

17 If the Lord were not to help me,
I would soon go down into the silence.

18 When I think: "I have lost my foothold";
your mercy, Lord, holds me up.
19 When cares increase in my heart
your consolation calms my soul.

20 Can judges who do evil be your friends?
They do injustice under cover of law;
21 they attack the life of the just
and condemn innocent blood.

22 As for me, the Lord will be a stronghold;
my God will be the rock where I take refuge.
23 He will repay them for their wickedness,
destroy them for their evil deeds.
The Lord, our God, will destroy them.

(94) 95. A call to praise and worship

1 Come, ring out our joy to the Lord;
hail the rock who saves us.
2 Let us come before him, giving thanks,
with songs let us hail the Lord.

3 A mighty God is the Lord,
a great king above all gods.
4 In his hands are the depths of the earth;
the heights of the mountains are his.
5 To him belongs the sea, for he made it
and the dry land shaped by his hands.

6 Come in; let us bow and bend low;
let us kneel before the God who made us
7 for he is our God and we
the people who belong to his pasture,
the flock that is led by his hand.

O that today you would listen to his voice!
8 "Harden not your hearts as at Meribah,
as on that day at Massah in the desert
9 when your forebears put me to the test;
when they tried me, though they saw my work.

10 For forty years I was wearied of these people
and I said: 'Their hearts are astray,
these people do not know my ways.'
11 Then I took an oath in my anger:
'Never shall they enter my rest.' "

(95) 96. God, king and judge of the world

1 O sing a new song to the Lord,
sing to the Lord all the earth.
2 O sing to the Lord, bless his name.

Proclaim his help day by day,
3 tell among the nations his glory
and his wonders among all the peoples.

4 The Lord is great and worthy of praise,
to be feared above all gods;
5 the gods of the heathens are naught.

It was the Lord who made the heavens,
6 his are majesty and state and power
and splendor in his holy place.

7 Give the Lord, you families of peoples,
give the Lord glory and power;
8 give the Lord the glory of his name.

Bring an offering and enter his courts,
9 worship the Lord in his temple.
O earth, tremble before him.

10 Proclaim to the nations: "God is king."
The world he made firm in its place;
he will judge the people in fairness.

11 Let the heavens rejoice and earth be glad,
let the sea and all within it thunder praise,
12 let the land and all it bears rejoice,
all the trees of the wood shout for joy

13 at the presence of the Lord for he comes,
he comes to rule the earth.
With justice he will rule the world,
he will judge the peoples with his truth.

(96) 97. Earth rejoices in its king

1 The Lord is king, let earth rejoice,
let all the coastlands be glad.
2 Cloud and darkness are his raiment;
his throne, justice and right.

3 A fire prepares his path;
it burns up his foes on every side.
4 His lightnings light up the world,
the earth trembles at the sight.

5 The mountains melt like wax
before the Lord of all the earth.
6 The skies proclaim his justice;
all peoples see his glory.

7 Let those who serve idols be ashamed,
those who boast of their worthless gods.
All you spirits, worship him.

8 Zion hears and is glad;
the people of Judah rejoice
because of your judgments, O Lord.

9 For you indeed are the Lord
most high above all the earth,
exalted far above all spirits.

10 The Lord loves those who hate evil;
he guards the souls of his saints;
he sets them free from the wicked.

11 Light shines forth for the just
and joy for the upright of heart.
12 Rejoice, you just, in the Lord;
give glory to his holy name.

(97) 98. Praise to God, ruler of the world

1 Sing a new song to the Lord
for he has worked wonders.
His right hand and his holy arm
have brought salvation.

2 The Lord has made known his salvation;
has shown his justice to the nations.

3 He has remembered his truth and love
for the house of Israel.

All the ends of the earth have seen
the salvation of our God.
4 Shout to the Lord, all the earth,
ring out your joy.

5 Sing psalms to the Lord with the harp
with the sound of music.
6 With trumpets and the sound of the horn
acclaim the King, the Lord.

* * * * *

7 Let the sea and all within it, thunder;
the world, and all its peoples.
8 Let the rivers clap their hands
and the hills ring out their joy

9 at the presence of the Lord, for he comes,
he comes to rule the earth.
He will rule the world with justice
and the peoples with fairness.

(98) 99. The power and holiness of God

1 The Lord is king; the peoples tremble.
He is throned on the cherubim; the earth quakes.
2 The Lord is great in Zion.

He is supreme over all the peoples.
3 Let them praise his name, so terrible and great,
he is holy, 4 full of power.

You are a king who loves what is right;
you have established equity, justice and right;
you have established them in Jacob.

5 Exalt the Lord our God;
bow down before Zion, his footstool.
He the Lord is holy.

6 Among his priests were Aaron and Moses,
among those who invoked his name was Samuel.
They invoked the Lord and he answered.

7 To them he spoke in the pillar of cloud.
They did his will; they kept the law,
which he, the Lord, had given.

8 O Lord our God, you answered them.
For them you were a God who forgives;
yet you punished all their offenses.

9 Exalt the Lord our God;
bow down before his holy mountain
for the Lord our God is holy.

(99) 100. Praise to God, creator and shepherd

1 Cry out with joy to the Lord, all the earth.
2 Serve the Lord with gladness.
Come before him, singing for joy.

3 Know that he, the Lord, is God.
He made us, we belong to him,
we are his people, the sheep of his flock.

4 Go within his gates, giving thanks.
Enter his courts with songs of praise.
Give thanks to him and bless his name.

5 Indeed, how good is the Lord,
eternal his merciful love.
He is faithful from age to age.

(100) 101. A mirror for rulers

1 My song is of mercy and justice;
I sing to you, O Lord.
2 I will walk in the way of perfection.
O when, Lord, will you come?

I will walk with blameless heart
within my house;
3 I will not set before my eyes
whatever is base.

I will hate the ways of the crooked;
they shall not be my friends.
4 The false-hearted must keep far away;
the wicked I disown.

5 Those who secretly slander their neighbors
I will bring to silence.
Those of proud look and haughty heart
I will never endure.

6 I look to the faithful in the land
that they may dwell with me.
Those who walk in the way of perfection
shall be my friends.

7 No one who practices deceit
shall live within my house.
No one who utters lies shall stand
before my eyes.

8 Morning by morning I will silence
all the wicked in the land,
uprooting from the city of the Lord
all who do evil.

(101) 102. Prayer for renewal: fifth psalm of repentance

2 O Lord, listen to my prayer
and let my cry for help reach you.
3 Do not hide your face from me
in the day of my distress.
Turn your ear towards me
and answer me quickly when I call.

4 For my days are vanishing like smoke,
my bones burn away like a fire.
5 My heart is withered like the grass.
I forget to eat my bread.
6 I cry with all my strength
and my skin clings to my bones.

7 I have become like a pelican in the wilderness
like an owl in desolate places.
8 I lie awake and I moan
like some lonely bird on a roof.
9 All day long my foes revile me;
those who hate me use my name as a curse.

10 The bread I eat is ashes;
my drink is mingled with tears.
11 In your anger, Lord, and your fury
you have lifted me up and thrown me down.
12 My days are like a passing shadow
and I wither away like the grass.

* * * * *

13 But you, O Lord, will endure for ever
and your name from age to age.
14 You will arise and have mercy on Zion:
for this is the time to have mercy,
(yes, the time appointed has come)
15 for your servants love her very stones,
are moved with pity even for her dust.

16 The nations shall fear the name of the Lord
and all the earth's kings your glory,
17 when the Lord shall build up Zion again
and appear in all his glory.
18 Then he will turn to the prayers of the helpless;
he will not despise their prayers.

19 Let this be written for ages to come
that a people yet unborn may praise the Lord;
20 for the Lord leaned down from his sanctuary
on high.
He looked down from heaven to the earth
21 that he might hear the groans of the prisoners
and free those condemned to die.

29 Our descendants shall dwell untroubled
and our children endure before you
22 that the name of the Lord may be proclaimed
in Zion
and his praise in the heart of Jerusalem,

23 when peoples and kingdoms are gathered
together
to pay their homage to the Lord.

* * * * *

24 He has broken my strength in mid-course;
he has shortened the days of my life.
25 I say to God: "Do not take me away
before my days are complete,
you, whose days last from age to age.

26 Long ago you founded the earth
and the heavens are the work of your hands.
27 They will perish but you will remain.
They will all wear out like a garment.
You will change them like clothes that are
changed.
28 But you neither change, nor have an end."

(102) 103. Praise of God's mercy and love

1 My soul, give thanks to the Lord
all my being, bless his holy name.
2 My soul, give thanks to the Lord
and never forget all his blessings.

3 It is he who forgives all your guilt,
who heals every one of your ills,
4 who redeems your life from the grave,
who crowns you with love and compassion,
5 who fills your life with good things,
renewing your youth like an eagle's.

6 The Lord does deeds of justice,
gives judgment for all who are oppressed.
7 He made known his ways to Moses
and his deeds to Israel's children.

8 The Lord is compassion and love,
slow to anger and rich in mercy.
9 His wrath will come to an end;
he will not be angry for ever.
10 He does not treat us according to our sins
nor repay us according to our faults.

11 For as the heavens are high above the earth
so strong is his love for those who fear him.
12 As far as the east is from the west
so far does he remove our sins.

13 As parents have compassion on their children,
the Lord has pity on those who fear him;
14 for he knows of what we are made,
he remembers that we are dust.

15 As for us, our days are like grass;
we flower like the flower of the field;
16 the wind blows and we are gone
and our place never sees us again.

17 But the love of the Lord is everlasting
upon those who hold him in fear;
his justice reaches out to children's children
18 when they keep his covenant in truth,
when they keep his will in their mind.

19 The Lord has set his sway in heaven
and his kingdom is ruling over all.
20 Give thanks to the Lord, all his angels,
mighty in power, fulfilling his word,
who heed the voice of his word.

21 Give thanks to the Lord, all his hosts,
his servants who do his will.
22 Give thanks to the Lord, all his works,
in every place where he rules.
My soul, give thanks to the Lord!

(103) 104. In praise of God the Creator

1 Bless the Lord, my soul!
Lord God, how great you are,
clothed in majesty and glory,
2 wrapped in light as in a robe!

* * * * *

You stretch out the heavens like a tent.
3 Above the rains you build your dwelling.
You make the clouds your chariot,
you walk on the wings of the wind;
4 you make the winds your messengers
and flashing fire your servants.

5 You founded the earth on its base,
to stand firm from age to age.
6 You wrapped it with the ocean like a cloak:
the waters stood higher than the mountains.

7 At your threat they took to flight;
at the voice of your thunder they fled.
8 They rose over the mountains and flowed down
to the place which you had appointed.
9 You set limits they might not pass
lest they return to cover the earth.

10 You make springs gush forth in the valleys;
they flow in between the hills.
11 They give drink to all the beasts of the field;
the wild asses quench their thirst.
12 On their banks dwell the birds of heaven;
from the branches they sing their song.

13 From your dwelling you water the hills;
earth drinks its fill of your gift.
14 You make the grass grow for the cattle
and the plants to serve our needs,

that we may bring forth bread from the earth
15 and wine to cheer our hearts;
oil, to make our faces shine
and bread to strengthen our hearts.

16 The trees of the Lord drink their fill,
the cedars he planted on Lebanon;
17 there the birds build their nests;
on the treetop the stork has her home.
18 The goats find a home on the mountains
and rabbits hide in the rocks.

19 You made the moon to mark the months;
the sun knows the time for its setting.
20 When you spread the darkness it is night
and all the beasts of the forest creep forth.
21 The young lions roar for their prey
and ask their food from God.

22 At the rising of the sun they steal away
and go to rest in their dens.
23 Men and women go out to their work,
to labor till evening falls.

24 How many are your works, O Lord!
In wisdom you have made them all.
The earth is full of your riches.

25 There is the sea, vast and wide,
with its moving swarms past counting,
living things great and small.
26 The ships are moving there
and the monsters you made to play with.

27 All of these look to you
to give them their food in due season.
28 You give it, they gather it up;
you open your hand, they have their fill.

29 You hide your face, they are dismayed;
you take back your spirit, they die,
returning to the dust from which they came.
30 You send forth your spirit, they are created;
and you renew the face of the earth.

31 May the glory of the Lord last for ever!
May the Lord rejoice in his works!
32 He looks on the earth and it trembles;
the mountains send forth smoke at his touch.

33 I will sing to the Lord all my life,
make music to my God while I live.
34 May my thoughts be pleasing to him.
I find my joy in the Lord.
35 Let sinners vanish from the earth
and the wicked exist no more.

Bless the Lord, my soul.

(104) 105. God's faithfulness to his promise: the story of Israel

Alleluia!

1 Give thanks to the Lord, tell his name,
make known his deeds among the peoples.

2 O sing to him, sing his praise;
tell all his wonderful works!
3 Be proud of his holy name,
let the hearts that seek the Lord rejoice.

4 Consider the Lord and his strength;
constantly seek his face.
5 Remember the wonders he has done,
his miracles, the judgements he spoke.

6 O children of Abraham, his servant,
O children of the Jacob he chose,
7 he, the Lord, is our God;
his judgments prevail in all the earth.

8 He remembers his covenant for ever,
his promise for a thousand generations,
9 the covenant he made with Abraham,
the oath he swore to Isaac.

10 He confirmed it for Jacob as a law,
for Israel as a covenant for ever.
11 He said: "I am giving you a land,
Canaan, your appointed heritage."

12 When they were few in number,
a handful of strangers in the land,
13 when they wandered from country to country,
from one kingdom and nation to another,

14 he allowed no one to oppress them;
he admonished kings on their account:
15 "Do not touch those I have anointed;
do no harm to any of my prophets."

16 But he called down a famine on the land;
he broke the staff that supported them.
17 He had sent a man before them,
Joseph, sold as a slave.

18 His feet were put in chains,
his neck was bound with iron,
19 until what he said came to pass
and the word of the Lord proved him true.

20 Then the king sent and released him;
the ruler of the peoples set him free,
21 making him master of his house
and ruler of all he possessed,

22 to instruct his princes as he pleased
and to teach his elders wisdom.
23 So Israel came into Egypt;
Jacob lived in the country of Ham.

24 He gave his people increase;
he made them stronger than their foes,
25 whose hearts he turned to hate his people
and to deal deceitfully with his servants.

26 Then he sent Moses his servant
and Aaron the man he had chosen.
27 Through them he showed his marvels
and his wonders in the country of Ham.

28 He sent darkness, and dark was made
but Egypt resisted his words.
29 He turned the waters into blood
and caused their fish to die.

30 Their land was alive with frogs,
even to the halls of their kings.
31 He spoke; the dogfly came
and gnats covered the land.

32 He sent hailstones in place of the rain
and flashing fire in their land.
33 He struck their vines and fig trees;
he shattered the trees through their land.

34 He spoke; the locusts came,
young locusts, too many to be counted.
35 They ate up every blade in the land;
they ate up all the fruit of their fields.

36 He struck all the first-born in their land,
the finest flower of their children.
37 He led out Israel with silver and gold.
Among the tribes were none who fell behind.

38 Egypt rejoiced when they left
for dread had fallen upon them.
39 He spread a cloud as a screen
and fire to give light in the darkness.

40 When they asked for food he sent quails;
he filled them with bread from heaven.
41 He pierced the rock to give them water;
it gushed forth in the desert like a river.

42 For he remembered his holy word,
which he gave to Abraham his servant.
43 So he brought out his people with joy,
his chosen ones with shouts of rejoicing.

44 And he gave them the land of the nations.
They took the fruit of other's toil,
45 that thus they might keep his precepts,
that thus they might observe his laws.

Alleluia!

(105) 106. The ingratitude of God's people

1 Alleluia!

O give thanks to the Lord for he is good;
for his love endures for ever.
2 Who can tell the Lord's mighty deeds?
Who can recount all his praise?

3 They are happy who do what is right,
who at all times do what is just.
4 O Lord, remember me
out of the love you have for your people.

Come to me, Lord, with your help
5 that I may see the joy of your chosen ones
and may rejoice in the gladness of your nation
and share the glory of your people.

6 Our sin is the sin of our forebears;
we have done wrong, our deeds have been evil.
7 Our forebears when they were in Egypt
paid no heed to your wonderful deeds.

They forgot the greatness of your love,
at the Red Sea defied the Most High.
8 Yet he saved them for the sake of his name,
in order to make known his power.

9 He threatened the Red Sea; it dried up
and he led them through the deep as through
the desert.
10 He saved them from the hand of the foe;
he saved them from the grip of the enemy.

11 The waters covered their oppressors;
not one of them was left alive.
12 Then they believed in his words:
then they sang his praises.

13 But they soon forgot his deeds
and would not wait upon his will.
14 They yielded to their cravings in the desert
and put God to the test in the wilderness.

15 He granted them the favor they asked
and sent disease among them.
16 Then they rebelled, envious of Moses
and of Aaron, who was holy to the Lord.

17 The earth opened and swallowed up Dathan
and buried the clan of Abiram.
18 Fire blazed up against their clan
and flames devoured the rebels.

19 They fashioned a calf at Horeb
and worshipped an image of metal,
20 exchanging the God who was their glory
for the image of a bull that eats grass.

21 They forgot the God who was their savior,
who had done such great things in Egypt,
22 such portents in the land of Ham,
such marvels at the Red Sea.

23 For this he said he would destroy them,
but Moses, the man he had chosen,
stood in the breach before him,
to turn back his anger from destruction.

24 Then they scorned the land of promise;
they had no faith in his word.
25 They complained inside their tents
and would not listen to the voice of the Lord.

26 So he raised his hand to swear an oath
that he would lay them low in the desert;
27 would scatter their children among the nations
and disperse them throughout the lands.

28 They bowed before the Baal of Peor;
ate offerings made to lifeless gods.
29 They roused him to anger with their deeds
and a plague broke out among them.

30 Then Phinehas stood up and intervened.
Thus the plague was ended
31 and this was counted in his favor
from age to age for ever.

32 They provoked him at the waters of Meribah.
Through their fault it went ill with Moses;
33 for they made his heart grow bitter
and he uttered words that were rash.

34 They failed to destroy the peoples
as the Lord had given command,
35 but instead they mingled with the nations
and learned to act as they did.

36 They worshipped the idols of the nations
and these became a snare to entrap them.
37 They even offered their own sons
and their daughters in sacrifice to demons.

38 They shed the blood of the innocent,
the blood of their sons and daughters
whom they offered to the idols of Canaan.
The land was polluted with blood.

39 So they defiled themselves by their deeds
and broke their marriage bond with the Lord
40 till his anger blazed against his people;
he was filled with horror at his chosen ones.

41 So he gave them into the hand of the nations
and their foes become their rulers.
42 Their enemies became their oppressors;
they were subdued beneath their hand.

43 Time after time God rescued them,
but in their malice they dared to defy him
and sank low through their guilt.
44 In spite of this he paid heed to their distress,
so often as he heard their cry.

45 For their sake he remembered his covenant.
In the greatness of his love he relented
46 and he let them be treated with mercy
by all who held them captive.

47 O Lord, our God, save us!
Bring us together from among the nations
that we may thank your holy name
and make it our glory to praise you.

* * * * *

48 Blessed be the Lord, God of Israel,
for ever, from age to age.
Let all the people cry out:
"Amen! Amen! Alleluia!"

(106) 107. God's inexhaustible love

1 "O give thanks to the Lord for he is good;
for his love endures for ever."

2 Let them say this, the Lord's redeemed,
whom he redeemed from the hand of the foe
3 and gathered from far-off lands,
from east and west, north and south.

* * * * *

4 Some wandered in the desert, in the wilderness,
finding no way to a city they could dwell in.
5 Hungry they were and thirsty;
their soul was fainting within them.

6 Then they cried to the Lord in their need
and he rescued them from their distress
7 and he led them along the right way,
to reach a city they could dwell in.

8 Let them thank the Lord for his love,
for the wonders he does for his people:
9 for he satisfies the thirsty soul;
he fills the hungry with good things.

* * * * *

10 Some lay in darkness and in gloom,
prisoners in misery and chains,
11 having defied the words of God
and spurned the counsels of the Most High.
12 He crushed their spirit with toil;
they stumbled; there was no one to help.

13 Then they cried to the Lord in their need
and he rescued them from their distress.
14 He led them forth from darkness and gloom
and broke their chains to pieces.

15 Let them thank the Lord for his goodness,
for the wonders he does for his people,
16 for he bursts the gates of bronze
and shatters the iron bars.

* * * * *

17 Some were sick on account of their sins
and afflicted on account of their guilt.
18 They had a loathing for every food;
they came close to the gates of death.

19 Then they cried to the Lord in their need
and he rescued them from their distress.
20 He sent forth his word to heal them
and saved their life from the grave.

21 Let them thank the Lord for his love,
for the wonders he does for his people.
22 Let them offer a sacrifice of thanks
and tell of his deeds with rejoicing.

* * * * *

23 Some sailed to the sea in ships
to trade on the mighty waters.
24 These men have seen the Lord's deeds,
the wonders he does in the deep.

25 For he spoke; he summoned the gale,
tossing the waves of the sea
26 up to heaven and back into the deep;
their souls melted away in their distress.

27 They staggered, reeled like drunkards,
for all their skill was gone.
28 Then they cried to the Lord in their need
and he rescued them from their distress.

29 He stilled the storm to a whisper;
all the waves of the sea were hushed.
30 They rejoiced because of the calm
and he led them to the haven they desired.

31 Let them thank the Lord for his love,
for the wonders he does for his people.
32 Let them exalt him in the gathering of the people
and praise him in the meeting of the elders.

* * * * *

33 He changes streams into a desert,
springs of water into thirsty ground,
34 fruitful land into a salty waste,
for the wickedness of those who live there.

35 But he changes desert into streams,
thirsty ground into springs of water.
36 There he settles the hungry
and they build a city to dwell in.

37 They sow fields and plant their vines;
these yield crops for the harvest.
38 He blesses them; they grow in numbers.
He does not let their herds decrease.

* * * * *

40 He pours contempt upon rulers,
makes them wander in trackless wastes.
39 They diminish, are reduced to nothing
by oppression, evil and sorrow.

41 But he raises the needy from distress;
makes families numerous as a flock.
42 The upright see it and rejoice
but all who do wrong are silenced.

43 Let those who are wise observe these things.
Let them ponder the love of the Lord.

(107) 108. A confident prayer for victory

2 My heart is ready, O God;
I will sing, sing your praise.

Awake, my soul;
3 awake, lyre and harp,
I will awake the dawn.

4 I will thank you, Lord, among the peoples,
among the nations I will praise you,
5 for your love reaches to the heavens
and your truth to the skies.
6 O God, arise above the heavens;
may your glory shine on earth!

7 O come and deliver your friends;
help with your right hand and reply.
8 From his holy place God has made this promise:
"I will triumph and divide the land of Shechem;
I will measure out the valley of Succoth.

9 Gilead is mine and Manasseh.
Ephraim I take for my helmet,
Judah for my commander's staff.
10 Moab I will use for my washbowl,
on Edom I will plant my shoe.
Over the Philistines I will shout in triumph."

11 But who will lead me to conquer the fortress?
Who will bring me face to face with Edom?
12 Will you utterly reject us, O God,
and no longer march with our armies?

13 Give us help against the foe,
for human help is vain.
14 With God we shall do bravely
and he will trample down our foes.

See Psalm (59) 60

(108) 109. Appeal for help against vicious enemies

1 O God whom I praise, do not be silent,
2 for the mouths of deceit and wickedness
are opened against me.

3 They speak to me with lying tongues;
they beset me with words of hate
and attack me without cause.

4 In return for my love they accuse me
while I pray for them.
5 They repay me evil for good,
hatred for love.

* * * * *

6 Appoint someone wicked as their judge;
let an accuser stand at their right.
7 When they are judged let them come out
condemned;
let their prayer be considered as sin.

8 Let the days of their life be few;
let others take their office.
9 Let their children lose father and mother
and their spouses know bereavement.

10 Let their children be wanderers and beggars
driven from the ruins of their home.
11 Let creditors seize all their goods;
let strangers take the fruit of their work.

12 Let no one show them mercy
nor pity their orphaned children.
13 Let their sons and daughters be destroyed
and with them their names be blotted out.

14 Let their fathers' guilt be remembered,
and the sins of their mothers retained.
15 Let these always stand before the Lord,
that their memory be cut off from the earth.

16 For they did not think of showing mercy
but pursued the poor and the needy,
hounding the wretched to death.
17 They loved cursing; let curses fall on them.
They scorned blessing; let blessing pass them by.

18 They put on cursing like a coat;
let it sink into their bodies like water;
let it sink like oil into their bones;
19 let it be like the clothes that cover them,
like a belt they cannot take off!

* * * * *

20 Let the Lord thus repay my accusers,
all those who speak evil against me.
21 For your name's sake act in my defense;
in the goodness of your love be my rescuer.

22 For I am poor and needy
and my heart is pierced within me.
23 I fade like an evening shadow;
I am shaken off like a locust.

24 My knees are weak from fasting;
my body is thin and gaunt.
25 I have become an object of scorn,
all who see me toss their heads.

26 Help me, Lord my God;
save me because of your love.

27 Let them know that this is your work,
that this is your doing, O Lord.

28 They may curse but you will bless.
Let my attackers be put to shame,
but let your servant rejoice.
29 Let my accusers be clothed with dishonor,
covered with shame as with a cloak.

30 Loud thanks to the Lord are on my lips.
I will praise him in the midst of the throng,
31 for God stands at the side of the poor
to save them from unjust condemnation.

(109) 110. The Lord and his chosen king

1 The Lord's revelation to my Master:
"Sit on my right;
your foes I will put beneath your feet."

2 The Lord will wield from Zion
your scepter of power;
rule in the midst of all your foes.

3 A prince from the day of your birth
on the holy mountains;
from the womb before the dawn I begot you.

4 The Lord has sworn an oath he will not change.
"You are a priest for ever,
a priest like Melchizedek of old."

* * * * *

5 The Master standing at your right hand
will shatter rulers in the day of his wrath.

6 He, the Judge of the nations,
will heap high the bodies;
heads shall be scattered far and wide.

7 He shall drink from the stream by the wayside
and therefore he shall lift up his head.

(110) 111. The great deeds of God

1 Alleluia!

I will thank the Lord with all my heart
in the meeting of the just and their assembly.
2 Great are the works of the Lord,
to be pondered by all who love them.

3 Majestic and glorious his work,
his justice stands firm for ever.
4 He makes us remember his wonders.
The Lord is compassion and love.

5 He gives food to those who fear him;
keeps his covenant ever in mind.
6 He has shown his might to his people
by giving them the land of the nations.

7 His works are justice and truth,
his precepts are all of them sure,
8 standing firm for ever and ever;
they are made in uprightness and truth.

9 He has sent deliverance to his people
and established his covenant for ever.
Holy his name, to be feared.

10 To fear the Lord is the first stage of wisdom;
all who do so prove themselves wise.
His praise shall last for ever!

(111) 112. The happiness of good people

1 Alleluia!
Happy are those who fear the Lord,
who take delight in all his commands.
2 Their descendants shall be powerful on earth;
the children of the upright are blessed.

3 Wealth and riches are in their homes;
their justice stands firm for ever.
4 They are lights in the darkness for the upright;
they are generous, merciful and just.

5 Good people take pity and lend,
they conduct their affairs with honor.
6 The just will never waver,
they will be remembered for ever.

7 They have no fear of evil news;
with firm hearts they trust in the Lord.
8 With steadfast hearts they will not fear;
they will see the downfall of their foes.

9 Openhanded, they give to the poor;
their justice stands firm for ever.
Their heads will be raised in glory.

10 The wicked shall see this and be angry,
shall grind their teeth and pine away;
the desires of the wicked lead to doom.

(112) 113. In praise of God's goodness

1 Alleluia!

Praise, O servants of the Lord,
praise the name of the Lord!
2 May the name of the Lord be blessed
both now and for evermore!
3 From the rising of the sun to its setting
praised be the name of the Lord!

4 High above all nations is the Lord,
above the heavens his glory.
5 Who is like the Lord, our God,
who has risen on high to his throne
6 yet stoops from the heights to look down,
to look down upon heaven and earth?

7 From the dust he lifts up the lowly,
from the dungheap he raises the poor
8 to set them in the company of rulers,
yes, with the rulers of his people.
9 To the childless wife he gives a home
and gladdens her heart with children.

(113A) 114. The wonders of the Exodus: the one true God

Alleluia!

When Israel came forth from Egypt,
Jacob's family from an alien people,
2 Judah became the Lord's temple,
Israel became his kingdom.

3 The sea fled at the sight,
the Jordan turned back on its course,
4 the mountains leapt like rams
and the hills like yearling sheep.

5 Why was it, sea, that you fled,
that you turned back, Jordan, on your course?
6 Mountains, that you leapt like rams;
hills, like yearling sheep?

7 Tremble, O earth, before the Lord,
in the presence of the God of Jacob,
8 who turns the rock into a pool
and flint into a spring of water.

(113B) 115. God and the idols

1 Not to us, Lord, not to us,
but to your name give the glory
for the sake of your love and your truth,
2 lest the heathen say: "Where is their God?"

3 But our God is in the heavens;
he does whatever he wills.
4 Their idols are silver and gold,
the work of human hands.

5 They have mouths but they cannot speak;
they have eyes but they cannot see;
6 they have ears but they cannot hear;
they have nostrils but they cannot smell.

7 With their hands they cannot feel;
with their feet they cannot walk.
(No sound comes from their throats.)

8 Their makers will come to be like them
and so will all who trust in them.

9 Israel's family, trust in the Lord;
he is their help and their shield.
10 Aaron's family, trust in the Lord;
he is their help and their shield.

11 You who fear him, trust in the Lord;
he is their help and their shield.
12 He remembers us, and he will bless us;
he will bless the family of Israel.
(He will bless the family of Aaron.)

13 The Lord will bless those who fear him,
the little no less than the great;
14 to you may the Lord grant increase,
to you and all your children.

15 May you be blessed by the Lord,
the maker of heaven and earth.
16 The heavens belong to the Lord
but to us he has given the earth.

17 The dead shall not praise the Lord,
nor those who go down into the silence.
18 But we who live bless the Lord
now and for ever. Amen.

(114) 116. Prayer of one saved from death

1 Alleluia!

I love the Lord for he has heard
the cry of my appeal;

2 for he turned his ear to me
in the day when I called him.

3 They surrounded me, the snares of death,
with the anguish of the tomb;
they caught me, sorrow and distress.
4 I called on the Lord's name.

O Lord, my God, deliver me!

5 How gracious is the Lord, and just;
our God has compassion.
6 The Lord protects the simple hearts;
I was helpless so he saved me.

7 Turn back, my soul, to your rest
for the Lord has been good;
8 he has kept my soul from death,
(my eyes from tears,)
my feet from stumbling.

9 I will walk in the presence of the Lord
in the land of the living.

(115). A promise in gratitude to God

10 I trusted, even when I said:
"I am sorely afflicted,"
11 and when I said in my alarm:
"There is no one I can trust."

12 How can I repay the Lord
for his goodness to me?
13 The cup of salvation I will raise;
I will call on the Lord's name.

14 My vows to the Lord I will fulfill
before all his people.
15 O precious in the eyes of the Lord
is the death of his faithful.

16 Your servant, Lord, your servant am I;
you have loosened my bonds.
17 A thanksgiving sacrifice I make;
I will call on the Lord's name.

18 My vows to the Lord I will fulfill
before all his people,
19 in the courts of the house of the Lord,
in your midst, O Jerusalem.

(116) 117. In praise to the Lord

1 Alleluia!

O praise the Lord, all you nations,
acclaim him all you peoples!

2 Strong is his love for us;
he is faithful for ever.

(117) 118. A processional song of praise

1 Alleluia!

Give thanks to the Lord for he is good,
for his love endures for ever.

2 Let the family of Israel say:
"His love endures for ever."
3 Let the family of Aaron say:
"His love endures for ever."
4 Let those who fear the Lord say:
"His love endures for ever."

5 I called to the Lord in my distress;
he answered and freed me.
6 The Lord is at my side; I do not fear.
What can mortals do against me?
7 The Lord is at my side as my helper;
I shall look down on my foes.

8 It is better to take refuge in the Lord
than to trust in mortals;
9 it is better to take refuge in the Lord
than to trust in rulers.

10 The nations all encompassed me;
in the Lord's name I crushed them.
11 They compassed me, compassed me about;
in the Lord's name I crushed them.
12 They compassed me about like bees;
they blazed like a fire among the thorns.
In the Lord's name I crushed them.

13 I was thrust down, thrust down and falling,
but the Lord was my helper.
14 The Lord is my strength and my song;
he was my savior.
15 There are shouts of joy and victory
in the tents of the just.

The Lord's right hand has triumphed;
16 his right hand raised me.
The Lord's right hand has triumphed;
17 I shall not die, I shall live
and recount his deeds.
18 I was punished, I was punished by the Lord,
but not doomed to die.

19 Open to me the gates of holiness:
I will enter and give thanks.
20 This is the Lord's own gate
where the just may enter.
21 I will thank you for you have answered
and you are my savior.

22 The stone which the builders rejected
has become the corner stone.
23 This is the work of the Lord,
a marvel in our eyes.
24 This day was made by the Lord;
we rejoice and are glad.

25 O Lord, grant us salvation;
O Lord, grant success.
26 Blessed in the name of the Lord
is the one who comes.
We bless you from the house of the Lord;
27 the Lord God is our light.

Go forward in procession with branches
even to the altar.
28 You are my God, I thank you.
My God, I praise you.
29 Give thanks to the Lord for he is good;
for his love endures for ever.

(118) 119. The law of the Lord

Aleph

1 They are happy whose life is blameless,
who follow God's law!
2 They are happy who do his will,
seeking him with all their hearts,
3 who never do anything evil
but walk in his ways.
4 You have laid down your precepts
to be obeyed with care.
5 May my footsteps be firm
to obey your statutes.
6 Then I shall not be put to shame
as I heed your commands.
7 I will thank you with an upright heart
as I learn your decrees.
8 I will obey your statutes;
do not forsake me.

Beth

9 How shall the young remain sinless?
By obeying your word.
10 I have sought you with all my heart;
let me not stray from your commands.
11 I treasure your promise in my heart
lest I sin against you.
12 Blessed are you, O Lord;
teach me your statutes.
13 With my tongue I have recounted
the decrees of your lips.
14 I rejoiced to do your will
as though all riches were mine.

15 I will ponder all your precepts
and consider your paths.
16 I take delight in your statutes;
I will not forget your word.

Gimmel

17 Bless your servant and I shall live
and obey your word.
18 Open my eyes that I may see
the wonders of your law.
19 I am a pilgrim on the earth;
show me your commands.
20 My soul is ever consumed
as I long for your decrees.
21 You threaten the proud, the accursed,
who turn from your commands.
22 Relieve me from scorn and contempt
for I do your will.
23 Though the powerful sit plotting against me
I ponder on your statutes.
24 Your will is my delight;
your statutes are my counsellors.

Daleth

25 My soul lies in the dust;
by your word revive me.
26 I declared my ways and you answered;
teach me your statutes.
27 Make me grasp the way of your precepts
and I will muse on your wonders.
28 My soul pines away with grief;
by your word raise me up.
29 Keep me from the way of error
and teach me your law.

30 I have chosen the way of truth
with your decrees before me.
31 I bind myself to do your will;
Lord, do not disappoint me.
32 I will run the way of your commands;
you give freedom to my heart.

He

33 Teach me the demands of your statutes
and I will keep them to the end.
34 Train me to observe your law,
to keep it with my heart.
35 Guide me in the path of your commands;
for there is my delight.
36 Bend my heart to your will
and not to love of gain.
37 Keep my eyes from what is false;
by your word, give me life.
38 Keep the promise you have made
to the servant who fears you.
39 Keep me from the scorn I dread,
for your decrees are good.
40 See, I long for your precepts;
then in your justice, give me life.

Vau

41 Lord, let your love come upon me,
the saving help of your promise.
42 And I shall answer those who taunt me
for I trust in your word.
43 Do not take the word of truth from my mouth
for I trust in your decrees.
44 I shall always keep your law
for ever and ever.

45 I shall walk in the path of freedom
for I seek your precepts.
46 I will speak of your will before the powerful
and not be abashed.
47 Your commands have been my delight;
these I have loved.
48 I will worship your commands and love them
and ponder your statutes.

Zayin

49 Remember your word to your servant
by which you gave me hope.
50 This is my comfort in sorrow:
that your promise gives me life.
51 Though the proud may utterly deride me
I keep to your law.
52 I remember your decrees of old
and these, Lord, console me.
53 I am seized with indignation at the wicked
who forsake your law.
54 Your statutes have become my song
in the land of exile.
55 I think of your name in the nighttime
and I keep your law.
56 This has been my blessing,
the keeping of your precepts.

Heth

57 My part, I have resolved, O Lord,
is to obey your word.
58 With all my heart I implore your favor;
show the mercy of your promise.
59 I have pondered over many ways
and returned to your will.

60 I made haste and did not delay
to obey your commands.
61 Though the nets of the wicked ensnared me
I remembered your law.
62 At midnight I will rise and thank you
for your just decrees.
63 I am a friend of all who revere you,
who obey your precepts.
64 Lord, your love fills the earth.
Teach me your statutes.

Teth

65 Lord, you have been good to your servant
according to your word.
66 Teach me discernment and knowledge
for I trust in your commands.
67 Before I was afflicted I strayed
but now I keep your word.
68 You are good and your deeds are good;
teach me your statutes.
69 Though the proud smear me with lies
yet I keep your precepts.
70 Their minds are closed to good
but your law is my delight.
71 It was good for me to be afflicted,
to learn your statutes.
72 The law from your mouth means more to me
then silver and gold.

Yod

73 It was your hands that made me and shaped me:
help me to learn your commands.
74 Your faithful will see me and rejoice
for I trust in your word.

75 Lord, I know that your decrees are right,
that you afflicted me justly.
76 Let your love be ready to console me
by your promise to your servant.
77 Let your love come and I shall live
for your law is my delight.
78 Shame the proud who harm me with lies
while I ponder your precepts.
79 Let your faithful turn to me,
those who know your will.
80 Let my heart be blameless in your statutes
lest I be ashamed.

Caph

81 I yearn for your saving help;
I hope in your word.
82 My eyes yearn to see your promise.
When will you console me?
83 Though parched and exhausted with waiting
I remember your statutes.
84 How long must your servant suffer?
When will you judge my foes?
85 For me the proud have dug pitfalls,
against your law.
86 Your commands are all true; then help me
when lies oppress me.
87 They almost made an end of me on earth,
but I kept your precepts.
88 Because of your love give me life
and I will do your will.

Lamed

89 Your word, O Lord, for ever
stands firm in the heavens:

90 your truth lasts from age to age,
like the earth you created.
91 By your decree it endures to this day;
for all things serve you.
92 Had your law not been my delight
I would have died in my affliction.
93 I will never forget your precepts
for with them you give me life.
94 Save me, for I am yours
since I seek your precepts.
95 Though the wicked lie in wait to destroy me
yet I ponder your will.
96 I have seen that all perfection has an end
but your command is boundless.

Mem

97 Lord, how I love your law!
It is ever in my mind.
98 Your command makes me wiser than my foes;
for it is mine for ever.
99 I have more insight than all who teach me
for I ponder your will.
100 I have more understanding than the old
for I keep your precepts.
101 I turn my feet from evil paths
to obey your word.
102 I have not turned from your decrees;
you yourself have taught me.
103 Your promise is sweeter to my taste
than honey in the mouth.
104 I gain understanding from your precepts
and so I hate false ways.

Nun

105 Your word is a lamp for my steps
and a light for my path.
106 I have sworn and have made up my mind
to obey your decrees.
107 Lord, I am deeply afflicted;
by your word give me life.
108 Accept, Lord, the homage of my lips
and teach me your decrees.
109 Though I carry my life in my hands,
I remember your law.
110 Though the wicked try to ensnare me,
I do not stray from your precepts.
111 Your will is my heritage for ever,
the joy of my heart.
112 I set myself to carry out your statutes
in fullness, for ever.

Samech

113 I have no love for the halfhearted;
my love is for your law.
114 You are my shelter, my shield;
I hope in your word.
115 Leave me, you who do evil;
I will keep God's command.
116 If you uphold me by your promise I shall live;
let my hopes not be in vain.
117 Sustain me and I shall be saved
and ever observe your statutes.
118 You spurn all who swerve from your statutes;
their cunning is in vain.
119 You throw away the wicked like dross;
so I love your will.

120 I tremble before you in terror;
I fear your decrees.

Ayin

121 I have done what is right and just:
let me not be oppressed.
122 Vouch for the welfare of your servant
lest the proud oppress me.
123 My eyes yearn for your saving help
and the promise of your justice.
124 Treat your servant with love
and teach me your statutes.
125 I am your servant, give me knowledge;
then I shall know your will.
126 It is time for the Lord to act
for your law has been broken.
127 That is why I love your commands
more than finest gold,
128 why I rule my life by your precepts,
and hate false ways.

Pe

129 Your will is wonderful indeed;
therefore I obey it.
130 The unfolding of your word gives light
and teaches the simple.
131 I open my mouth and I sigh
as I yearn for your commands.
132 Turn and show me your mercy;
show justice to your friends.
133 Let my steps be guided by your promise;
let no evil rule me.
134 Redeem me from those who oppress me
and I will keep your precepts.

135 Let your face shine on your servant
and teach me your decrees.
136 Tears stream from my eyes
because your law is disobeyed.

Sade

137 Lord, you are just indeed;
your decrees are right.
138 You have imposed your will with justice
and with absolute truth.
139 I am carried away by anger
for my foes forget your word.
140 Your promise is tried in the fire,
the delight of your servant.
141 Although I am weak and despised,
I remember your precepts.
142 Your justice is eternal justice
and your law is truth.
143 Though anguish and distress have seized me,
I delight in your commands.
144 The justice of your will is eternal:
if you teach me I shall live.

Koph

145 I call with all my heart; Lord, hear me,
I will keep your statutes.
146 I call upon you, save me
and I will do your will.
147 I rise before dawn and cry for help,
I hope in your word.
148 My eyes watch through the night
to ponder your promise.
149 In your love hear my voice, O Lord;
give me life by your decrees.

150 Those who harm me unjustly draw near;
they are far from your law.
151 But you, O Lord, are close,
your commands are truth.
152 Long have I known that your will
is established for ever.

Resh

153 See my affliction and save me
for I remember your law.
154 Uphold my cause and defend me;
by your promise, give me life.
155 Salvation is far from the wicked
who are heedless of your statutes.
156 Numberless, Lord, are your mercies;
with your decrees give me life.
157 Though my foes and oppressors are countless
I have not swerved from your will.
158 I look at the faithless with disgust;
they ignore your promise.
159 See how I love your precepts;
in your mercy give me life.
160 Your word is founded on truth,
your decrees are eternal.

Shin

161 Though the powerful oppress me unjustly,
I stand in awe of your word.
162 I take delight in your promise
like one who finds a treasure.
163 Lies I hate and detest
but your law is my love.
164 Seven times a day I praise you
for your just decrees.

165 The lovers of your law have great peace;
they never stumble.
166 I await your saving help, O Lord,
I fulfill your commands.
167 My soul obeys your will
and loves it dearly.
168 I obey your precepts and your will;
all that I do is before you.

Tau

169 Lord, let my cry come before you:
teach me by your word.
170 Let my pleading come before you:
save me by your promise.
171 Let my lips proclaim your praise
because you teach me your statutes.
172 Let my tongue sing your promise
for your commands are just.
173 Let your hand be ready to help me,
since I have chosen your precepts.
174 Lord, I long for your saving help
and your law is my delight.
175 Give life to my soul that I may praise you.
Let your decrees give me help.
176 I am lost like a sheep; seek your servant
for I remember your commands.

(119) 120. Amongst treacherous strangers: a pilgrimage song

1 To the Lord in the hour of my distress
I call and he answers me.
2 "O Lord, save my soul from lying lips,
from the tongue of the deceitful."

3 What shall he pay you in return,
O treacherous tongue?
4 Arrows sharpened for war
and coals, red-hot, blazing.

5 (Alas, that I abide a stranger in Meshech,
dwell among the tents of Kedar!)
6 Long enough have I been dwelling
with those who hate peace.
7 I am for peace, but when I speak,
they are for fighting.

(120) 121. The Lord, our protector: a pilgrimage song

1 I lift up my eyes to the mountains;
from where shall come my help?
2 My help shall come from the Lord
who made heaven and earth.

3 My he never allow you to stumble!
Let him sleep not, your guard.
4 No, he sleeps not nor slumbers,
Israel's guard.

5 The Lord is your guard and your shade;
at your right side he stands.
6 By day the sun shall not smite you
nor the moon in the night.

7 The Lord will guard you from evil,
he will guard your soul.
8 The Lord will guard your going and coming
both now and for ever.

(121) 122. In praise of Jerusalem: a pilgrimage song

1 I rejoiced when I heard them say:
"Let us go to God's house."
2 And now our feet are standing
within your gates, O Jerusalem.

3 Jerusalem is built as a city
strongly compact.
4 It is there that the tribes go up,
the tribes of the Lord.

For Israel's law it is,
there to praise the Lord's name.
5 There were set the thrones of judgment
of the house of David.

6 For the peace of Jerusalem pray:
"Peace be to your homes!
7 May peace reign in your walls,
in your palaces, peace!"

8 For love of my family and friends
I say: "Peace upon you."
9 For love of the house of the Lord
I will ask for your good.

(122) 123. A prayer for mercy: a pilgrimage song

1 To you have I lifted up my eyes,
you who dwell in the heavens;
2 my eyes, like the eyes of slaves
on the hand of their lords.

Like the eyes of a servant
on the hand of her mistress,
3 so our eyes are on the Lord our God
till he show us his mercy.

4 Have mercy on us, Lord, have mercy.
We are filled with contempt.
5 Indeed all too full in our soul
with the scorn of the rich,
(the disdain of the proud).

(123) 124. Thanksgiving for protection: a pilgrimage song

1 "If the Lord had not been on our side,"
this is Israel's song.
2 "If the Lord had not been on our side
when they rose up against us,
3 then would they have swallowed us alive
when their anger was kindled.

4 Then would the waters have engulfed us,
the torrent gone over us;
5 over our head would have swept
the raging waters."

6 Blessed be the Lord who did not give us
a prey to their teeth!
7 Our life, like a bird, has escaped
from the snare of the fowler.

Indeed the snare has been broken
and we have escaped.
8 Our help is in the name of the Lord,
who made heaven and earth.

(124) 125. Unshakable trust: a pilgrimage song

1 Those who put their trust in the Lord
are like Mount Zion, that cannot be shaken,
that stands for ever.

2 Jerusalem! The mountains surround her,
so the Lord surrounds his people
both now and for ever.

3 For the scepter of the wicked shall not rest
over the land of the just
for fear that the hands of the just
should turn to evil.

4 Do good, Lord, to those who are good,
to the upright of heart;
5 but the crooked and those who do evil,
drive them away!

On Israel, peace!

(125) 126. Song of the returned exiles: a pilgrimage song

1 When the Lord delivered Zion from bondage,
it seemed like a dream.
2 Then was our mouth filled with laughter,
on our lips there were songs.

The heathens themselves said: "What marvels
the Lord worked for them!"
3 What marvels the Lord worked for us!
Indeed we were glad.

4 Deliver us, O Lord, from our bondage
as streams in dry land.
5 Those who are sowing in tears
will sing when they reap.

6 They go out, they go out, full of tears,
carrying seed for the sowing;
they come back, they come back, full of song,
carrying their sheaves.

(126) 127. Praise of God's goodness: a pilgrimage song

1 If the Lord does not build the house,
in vain do its builders labor;
if the Lord does not watch over the city,
in vain do the watchers keep vigil.

2 In vain is your earlier rising,
your going later to rest,
you who toil for the bread you eat,
when he pours gifts on his beloved while
they slumber.

3 Yes, children are a gift from the Lord,
a blessing, the fruit of the womb.
4 The sons and daughters of youth
are like arrows in the hand of a warrior.

5 O the happiness of those
who have filled their quiver with these arrows!
They will have no cause for shame
when they dispute with their foes in the
gateways.

(127) 128. The blessings of home: a pilgrimage song

1 O blessed are you who fear the Lord
and walk in his ways!

2 By the labor of your hands you shall eat.
You will be happy and prosper;
3 the wife like a fruitful vine
in the heart of the house;
children like shoots of the olive,
around the table.

4 Indeed thus shall the blessed
those who fear the Lord.
5 May the Lord bless you from Zion
5c all the days of your life!
6 May you see your children's children
5b in a happy Jerusalem!

On Israel, peace!

(128) 129. A prayer against Israel's enemies: a pilgrimage song

1 "They have pressed me hard from my youth,"
this is Israel's song.
2 "They have pressed me hard from my youth
but could never destroy me.

3 They plowed my back like plowmen,
drawing long furrows.
4 But the lord who is just, has destroyed
the yoke of the wicked."

5 Let them be shamed and routed,
those who hate Zion!
6 Let them be like grass on the roof
that withers before it flowers.

7 With that no reapers fill their arms,
no binders make their sheaves
8 and those passing by will not say:
"On you the Lord's blessing!"

"We bless you in the name of the Lord."

(129) 130. A prayer of repentance and trust: sixth psalm of repentance

1 Out of the depths I cry to you, O Lord,
2 Lord, hear my voice!
O let your ears be attentive
to the voice of my pleading.

3 If you, O Lord, should mark our guilt,
Lord, who would survive?
4 But with you is found forgiveness:
for this we revere you.

5 My soul is waiting for the Lord.
I count on his word.
6 My soul is longing for the Lord
more than those who watch for daybreak.
(Let the watchers count on daybreak
7 and Israel on the Lord.)

Because with the Lord there is mercy
and fullness of redemption,
8 Israel indeed he will redeem
from all its iniquity.

(130) 131. The peaceful heart: a pilgrimage song

1 O Lord, my heart is not proud
nor haughty my eyes.
I have not gone after things too great
nor marvels beyond me.

2 Truly I have set my soul
in silence and peace.
A weaned child on its mother's breast,
even so is my soul.

3 O Israel, hope in the Lord
both now and for ever.

(131) 132. God's promise to David: a pilgrimage song

1 O Lord, remember David
and all the many hardships he endured,
2 the oath he swore to the Lord,
his vow to the Strong One of Jacob.

3 "I will not enter the house where I live
nor go to the bed where I rest.
4 I will give no sleep to my eyes,
to my eyelids I will give no slumber
5 till I find a place for the Lord,
a dwelling for the Strong One of Jacob."

6 At Ephrata we heard of the ark;
we found it in the plains of Yearim.
7 "Let us go to the place of his dwelling;
let us go to kneel at his footstool."

8 Go up, Lord, to the place of your rest,
you and the ark of your strength.
9 Your priests shall be clothed with holiness;
your faithful shall ring out their joy.
10 For the sake of David your servant
do not reject your anointed.

11 The Lord swore an oath to David;
he will not go back on this word:
"A son, the fruit of your body,
will I set upon your throne.
12 If they keep my covenant in truth
and my laws that I have taught them,
their children too shall rule
on your throne from age to age."

13 For the Lord has chosen Zion;
he has desired it for his dwelling:
14 "This is my resting-place for ever,
here have I chosen to live.
15 I will greatly bless her produce,
I will fill her poor with bread.
16 I will clothe her priests with salvation
and her faithful shall ring out their joy.

17 There David's stock will flower;
I will prepare a lamp for my anointed.
18 I will cover his enemies with shame
but on him my crown shall shine."

(132) 133. The blessings of unity: a pilgrimage song

1 How good and how pleasant it is,
when people live in unity!

2 It is like precious oil upon the head
running down upon the beard,
running down upon Aaron's beard,
upon the collar of his robes.

3 It is like the dew of Hermon which falls
on the heights of Zion.
For there the Lord gives his blessing,
life for ever.

(133) 134. Prayer at nighttime: a pilgrimage song

1 O come, bless the Lord,
all you who serve the Lord,
who stand in the house of the Lord,
in the courts of the house of our God.

2 Lift up your hands to the holy place
and bless the Lord through the night.

3 May the Lord bless you from Zion,
he who made both heaven and earth.

(134) 135. A hymn of praise

1 Alleluia!

Praise the name of the Lord,
praise him, servants of the Lord,
2 who stand in the house of the Lord
in the courts of the house of our God.

3 Praise the Lord for the Lord is good.
Sing a psalm to his name for he is loving.
4 For the Lord has chosen Jacob for himself
and Israel for his own possession.

5 For I know the Lord is great,
that our Lord is high above all gods.
6 The Lord does whatever he wills,
in heaven, on earth, in the seas.

7 He summons clouds from the ends of the earth;
makes lightning produce the rain;
from his treasuries he sends forth the wind.

8 The first-born of the Egyptians he smote,
of humans and beasts alike.
9 Signs and wonders he worked
in the midst of your land, O Egypt,
against Pharaoh and all his servants.

10 Nations in their greatness he struck
and kings in their splendor he slew.
11 Sihon, king of the Amorites,
Og, the king of Bashan,
and all the kingdoms of Canaan.
12 He let Israel inherit their land;
on his people their land he bestowed.

13 Lord, your name stands for ever,
unforgotten from age to age,
14 for the Lord does justice for his people;
the Lord takes pity on his servants.

15 Pagans idols are silver and gold,
the work of human hands.
16 They have mouths but they cannot speak;
they have eyes but they cannot see.

17 They have ears but they cannot hear;
there is never a breath on their lips.
18 Their makers will come to be like them
and so will all who trust in them!

19 House of Israel, bless the Lord!
House of Aaron, bless the Lord!
20 House of Levi, bless the Lord!
You who fear him, bless the Lord!

21 From Zion may the Lord be blessed,
he who dwells in Jerusalem!

(135) 136. Litany of praises: psalm of worship

1 Alleluia!
O give thanks to the Lord for he is good,
for his love endures for ever.
2 Give thanks to the God of gods,
for his love endures for ever.
3 Give thanks to the Lord of lords,
for his love endures for ever;

4 who alone has wrought marvelous works,
for his love endures for ever;
5 whose wisdom it was made the skies,
for his love endures for ever;
6 who fixed the earth firmly on the seas,
for his love endures for ever.

7 It was he who made the great lights,
for his love endures for ever;
8 the sun to rule in the day,
for his love endures for ever;

9 the moon and stars in the night,
for his love endures for ever.

10 The first-born of the Egyptians he smote,
for his love endures for ever.
11 He brought Israel out form the midst,
for his love endures for ever;
12 arm outstretched, with power in his hand,
for his love endures for ever.

13 He divided the Red Sea in two,
for his love endures for ever;
14 he made Israel pass through the midst,
for his love endures for ever;
15 he flung Pharoah and his force in the sea,
for his love endures for ever.

16 Through the desert his people he led,
for his love endures for ever.
17 Nations in their greatness he struck,
for his love endures for ever.
18 Kings in their splendor he slew,
for his love endures for ever.

19 Sihon, king of the Amorites,
for his love endures for ever;
20 and Og, the king of Bashan,
for his love endures for ever.

21 He let Israel inherit their land,
for his love endures for ever.
22 On his servant their land he bestowed,
for his love endures for ever.
23 He remembered us in our distress,
for his love endures for ever.

24 And he snatched us away from our foes,
for his loves endures for ever.
25 He gives food to all living things,
for his loves endures for ever.
26 To the God of heaven give thanks,
for his love endures for ever.

(136) 137. Homesickness in exile

1 By the rivers of Babylon
there we sat and wept,
remembering Zion;
2 on the poplars that grew there
we hung up our harps.

3 For it was there that they asked us,
our captors, for songs,
our oppressors, for joy.
"Sing to us," they said,
"one of Zion's songs."

4 O how could we sing
the song of the Lord
on alien soil?
5 If I forget you, Jerusalem,
let my right hand wither!

6 O let my tongue
cleave to my mouth
if I remember you not,
if I prize not Jerusalem
above all my joys!

7 Remember, O Lord,
against the people of Edom
the day of Jerusalem;
when they said: "Tear it down!
Tear it down to its foundations!"

8 O Babylon, destroyer,
they are happy who repay you
the ills you brought on us.
9 They shall seize and shall dash
your children on the rock!

(137) 138. A song of deliverance

1 I thank you, Lord, with all my heart,
you have heard the words of my mouth.
In the presence of the angels I will bless you.
2 I will adore before you holy temple.

I thank you for your faithfulness and love
which excel all we ever knew of you.
3 On the day I called, you answered;
you increased the strength of my soul.

4 All the rulers on earth shall thank you
when they hear the words of your mouth.
5 They shall sing of the Lord's ways:
"How great is the glory of the Lord!"

6 The Lord is high yet he looks on the lowly
and the haughty he knows from afar.
7 Though I walk in the midst of affliction
you give me life and frustrate my foes.

You stretch out your hand and save me,
your hand 8 will do all things for me.
Your love, O Lord, is eternal,
discard not the work of your hands.

(138) 139. God's knowledge and care

1 O Lord, you search me and you know me,
2 you know my resting and my rising,
you discern my purpose from afar.
3 You mark when I walk or lie down,
all my ways lie open to you.

4 Before ever a word is on my tongue
you know it, O Lord, through and through.
5 Behind and before you besiege me,
your hand ever laid upon me.
6 Too wonderful for me, this knowledge,
too high, beyond my reach.

7 O where can I go from your spirit,
or where can I flee from your face?
8 If I climb the heavens, you are there.
If I lie in the grave, you are there.

9 If I take the wings of the dawn
and dwell at the sea's furthest end,
10 even there your hand would lead me,
your right hand would hold me fast.

11 If I say: "Let the darkness hide me
and the light around me be night,"
12 even darkness is not dark for you
and the night is as clear as the day.

13 For it was you who created my being,
knit me together in my mother's womb.
14 I thank you for the wonder of my being,
for the wonders of all your creation.

Already you knew my soul,
15 my body held no secret from you
when I was being fashioned in secret
and moulded in the depths of the earth.

16 Your eyes saw all my actions,
they were all of them written in your book;
every one of my days was decreed
before one of them came into being.

17 To me, how mysterious your thoughts,
the sum of them not to be numbered!
18 If I count them, they are more than the sand;
to finish, I must be eternal, like you.

19 O God, that you would slay the wicked!
Keep away from me, violent hands!
20 With deceit they rebel against you
and set your designs at naught.

21 Do I not hate those who hate you,
abhor those who rise against you?
22 I hate them with a perfect hate
and they are foes to me.

23 O search me, God, and know my heart.
O test me and know my thoughts.
24 See that I follow not the wrong path
and lead me in the path of life eternal.

(139) 140. A prayer for protection against enemies

2 Rescue me, Lord, from the wicked;
from the violent keep me safe,
3 from those who plan evil in their hearts
and stir up strife every day;
4 who sharpen their tongue like an adder's,
with the poison of viper on their lips.

5 Lord, guard me from the hands of the wicked;
from the violent keep me safe;
they plan to make me stumble.
6 The proud have hidden a trap,
have spread out lines in a net,
set snares across my path.

7 I have said to the Lord: "You are my God."
Lord, hear the cry of my appeal!
8 Lord my God, my mighty help,
you shield my head in the battle.
9 Do not grant the wicked their desire
nor let their plots succeed.

10 Those surrounding me lift up their heads.
Let the malice of their speech overwhelm them.
11 Let coals of fire rain upon them.
Let them be flung in the abyss, no more to rise.
12 Let slanderers not stand upon the earth.
Let the violent be hunted down by evil!

13 I know that you will avenge the poor,
and do justice, Lord, for the needy.
Yes, the just will praise your name;
the upright shall live in your presence.

(140) 141. An evening prayer for protection

1 I have called to you, Lord; hasten to help me!
Hear my voice when I cry to you.
2 Let my prayer arise before you like incense,
the raising of my hands like an evening oblation.

3 Set, O Lord, a guard over my mouth;
keep watch, O Lord, at the door of my lips!
4 Do not turn my heart to things that are wrong,
to evil deeds with those who are sinners.

Never allow me to share in their feasting.
5 If the upright strike or reprove me it is kindness;
but let the oil of the wicked not anoint my head.
Let my prayer be ever against their malice.

6 Their leaders were thrown down by the side
of the rock;
then they understood that my words were kind.
7 As a millstone is shattered to pieces on the
ground,
so their bones were strewn at the mouth of
the grave.

8 To you, Lord God, my eyes are turned;
in you I take refuge; spare my soul!
9 From the trap they have laid for me keep me safe;
keep me from the snares of those who do evil.

10 Let the wicked fall into the traps they have set
whilst I pursue my way unharmed.

(141) 142. The prayer of one deserted by friends

2 With all my voice I cry to you, Lord,
with all my voice I entreat you, Lord.
3 I pour out my trouble before you;
I tell you all my distress
4 while my spirit faints within me.
But you, O Lord, know my path.

On the way where I shall walk
they have hidden a snare to entrap me.
5 Look on my right and see:
there is no one who takes my part.
I have no means of escape,
not one who cares for my soul.

6 I cry to you, O Lord.
I have said: "You are my refuge,
all I have in the land of the living."
7 Listen, then, to my cry
for I am in the depths of distress.

Rescue me from those who pursue me
for they are stronger than I.
8 Bring my soul out of this prison
and then I shall praise your name.
Around me the just will assemble
because of your goodness to me.

(142) 143. A prayer in desolation: seventh psalm of repentance

1 Lord, listen to my prayer,
turn your ear to my appeal.
You are faithful, you are just; give answer.

2 Do not call your servant to judgment
for no one is just in your sight.

3 The enemy pursues my soul;
he has crushed my life to the ground;
he has made me dwell in darkness
like the dead, long forgotten.
4 Therefore my spirit fails;
my heart is numb within me.

5 I remember the days that are past;
I ponder all your works.
I muse on what your hand has wrought
6 and to you I stretch out my hands.
Like a parched land my soul thirsts for you.

7 Lord, make haste and answer;
for my spirit fails within me.
Do not hide your face
lest I become like those in the grave.

8 In the morning let me know your love
for I put my trust in you.
Make me know the way I should walk;
to you I lift up my soul.

9 Rescue me, Lord, from my enemies;
I have fled to you for refuge.
10 Teach me to do your will
for you, O Lord, are my God.
Let your good spirit guide me
in ways that are level and smooth.

11 For your name's sake, Lord, save my life;
in your justice save my soul from distress.

12 In your love make an end of my foes;
destroy all those who oppress me
for I am your servant, O Lord.

(143) 144. An appeal for victory and peace

1 Blessed be the Lord, my rock,
who trains my arms for battle,
who prepares my hands for war.

2 He is my love, my fortress;
he is my stronghold, my savior,
my shield, my place of refuge.
He brings peoples under my rule.

3 Lord, what are we that you care for us,
mere mortals, that you keep us in mind;
4 creatures, who are merely a breath
whose life fades like a shadow?

5 Lower your heavens and come down;
touch the mountains; wreathe them in smoke.
6 Flash your lightnings; rout the foe,
shoot your arrows and put them to flight.

7 Reach down from heaven and save me;
draw me out from the mighty waters,
from the hands of alien foes
8 whose mouths are filled with lies,
whose hands are raised in perjury.

9 To you, O God, will I sing a new song;
I will play on the ten-stringed lute
10 to you who give kings their victory,
who set David your servant free.

11 You set him free from the evil sword;
you rescued him from alien foes
whose mouths were filled with lies,
whose hands were raised in perjury.

* * * *

12 Let out sons then flourish like saplings
grown tall and strong from their youth,
our daughters graceful as columns,
adorned as though for a palace.

13 Let our barns be filled to overflowing
with crops of every kind;
our sheep increasing by thousands,
myriads of sheep in our fields,
14 our cattle heavy with young,

no ruined wall, no exile,
no sound of weeping in our streets.
15 Happy the people with such blessings;
happy the people whose God is the Lord.

(144) 145. Praise of God's glory

1 I will give you glory, O God my king,
I will bless your name for ever.

2 I will bless you day after day
and praise your name for ever.
3 You are great, Lord, highly to be praised,
your greatness cannot be measured.

4 Age to age shall proclaim your works,
shall declare your mighty deeds,

5 shall speak of your splendor and glory,
tell the tale of your wonderful works.
6 They will speak of your terrible deeds,
recount your greatness and might.
7 They will recall your abundant goodness;
age to age shall ring out your justice.

8 You are kind and full of compassion,
slow to anger, abounding in love.
9 How good you are, Lord, to all,
compassionate to all your creatures.

10 All your creatures shall thank you, O Lord,
and your friends shall repeat their blessing.
11 They shall speak of the glory of your reign
and declare your might, O God,

12 to make known to all your mighty deeds
and the glorious splendor of your reign.
13 Yours is an everlasting kingdom;
your rule lasts from age to age.

You are faithful in all your words
and loving in all your deeds.
14 You support all those who are falling
and raise up all who are bowed down.

15 The eyes of all creatures look to you
and you give them their food in due time.
16 You open wide your hand,
grant the desires of all who live.

17 You are just in all your ways
and loving in all your deeds.
18 You are close to all who call you,
who call on you from their hearts.

19 You grant the desires of those who fear you,
you hear their cry and you save them.
20 Lord, you protect all who love you;
but the wicked you will utterly destroy.

21 Let me speak your praise, O Lord,
let all peoples bless your holy name
for ever, for ages unending.

(145) 146. Praise of God's faithfulness

1 Alleluia!

My soul, give praise to the Lord;
2 I will praise the Lord all my days,
make music to my God while I live.

3 Put no trust in the powerful,
mere mortals in whom there is no help.
4 Take their breath, they return to clay
and their plans that day come to nothing.

5 They are happy who are helped by Jacob's God,
whose hope is in the Lord their God,
6 who alone made heaven and earth,
the seas and all they contain.

It is the Lord who keeps faith for ever,
7 who is just to those who are oppressed.
It is God who gives bread to the hungry,
the Lord, who sets prisoners free,

8 the Lord who gives sight to the blind,
who raises up those who are bowed down,

9 the Lord, who protects the stranger
and upholds the widow and orphan.

8c It is the Lord who loves the just
9c but thwarts the path of the wicked.
10 The Lord will reign for ever,
Zion's God, from age to age.

Alleluia!

(146) 147. A song of thanksgiving

1 Alleluia!

Praise the Lord for he is good;
sing to our God for he is loving:
to him our praise is due.

2 The Lord builds up Jerusalem
and brings back Israel's exiles,
3 he heals the broken-hearted,
he binds up all their wounds.
4 He fixes the number of the stars;
he calls each one by its name.

5 Our Lord is great and almighty;
his wisdom can never be measured.
6 The Lord raises the lowly;
he humbles the wicked to the dust.
7 O sing to the Lord, giving thanks;
sing psalms to our God with the harp.

8 He covers the heavens with clouds;
he prepares the rain for the earth,

making mountains sprout with grass
and with plants to serve our needs.
9 He provides the beasts with their food
and young ravens that call upon him.

10 His delight is not in horses
nor his pleasure in warriors' strength.
11 The Lord delights in those who revere him,
in those who wait for his love.

(147) 147B. In praise of God the Almighty

12 O praise the Lord, Jerusalem!
Zion, praise your God!

13 He has strengthened the bars of your gates,
he has blessed the children within you.
14 He established peace on your borders,
he feeds you with finest wheat.

15 He sends out his word to the earth
and swiftly runs his command.
16 He showers down snow white as wool,
he scatters hoarfrost like ashes.

17 He hurls down hailstones like crumbs.
The waters are frozen at his touch;
18 he sends forth his word and it melts them:
at the breath of his mouth the waters flow.

19 He makes his word known to Jacob,
to Israel his laws and decrees.
20 He has not dealt thus with other nations;
he has not taught them his decrees.

Alleluia!

148. Cosmic praise

1 Alleluia!

Praise the Lord from the heavens,
praise him in the heights.
2 Praise him, all his angels,
praise him, all his host.

3 Praise him, sun and moon,
praise him, shining stars.
4 Praise him, highest heavens
and the waters above the heavens.

5 Let them praise the name of the Lord.
He commanded: they were made.
6 He fixed them for ever,
gave a law which shall not pass away.

7 Praise the Lord from the earth,
sea creatures and all oceans,
8 fire and hail, snow and mist,
stormy winds that obey his word;

9 all mountains and hills,
all fruit trees and cedars,
10 beasts, wild and tame,
reptiles and birds on the wing;

11 all earth's nations and peoples,
earth's leaders and rulers;
12 young men and maidens,
the old together with children.

13 Let them praise the name of the Lord
for he alone is exalted.

The splendor of his name
reaches beyond heaven and earth.

14 He exalts the strength of his people.
He is the praise of all his saints,
of the sons and daughters of Israel,
of the people to whom he comes close.

Alleluia!

149. Praise to the God of victories

1 Alleluia!

Sing a new song to the Lord,
his praise in the assembly of the faithful.
2 Let Israel rejoice in its Maker,
let Zion's people exult in their king.
3 Let them praise his name with dancing
and make music with timbrel and harp.

4 For the Lord takes delight in his people.
He crowns the poor with salvation.
5 Let the faithful rejoice in their glory,
shout for joy and take their rest.
6 Let the praise of God be on their lips
and a two-edged sword in their hand,

7 to deal out vengeance to the nations
and punishment on all the peoples;
8 to bind their kings in chains
and their nobles in fetters of iron;
9 to carry out the sentence pre-ordained:
this honor is for all his faithful.

Alleluia!

150. Praise the Lord

1 Alleluia!

Praise God in his holy place,
praise him in his mighty heavens.
2 Praise him for his powerful deeds,
praise his surpassing greatness.

3 O praise him with sound of trumpet,
praise him with lute and harp.
4 Praise him with timbrel and dance,
praise him with strings and pipes.

5 O praise him with resounding cymbals,
praise him with clashing of cymbals.
6 Let everything that lives and that breathes
give praise to the Lord. Alleluia!